**Working with
Behavioral Disorders**

*M*OVING ON:

Transitions for Youth
with Behavioral Disorders

Michael Bullis
and Robert Gaylord-Ross

CEC   ERIC®

A Product of the ERIC Clearinghouse on Handicapped and Gifted Children
Published by The Council for Exceptional Children

Library of Congress Cataloging-in-Publication Data

Bullis, Michael.
    Moving on : transitions for youth with behavioral disorders /
Michael Bullis, Robert Gaylord-Ross.
        p.   cm. — (Working with behavioral disorders)
    "CEC mini-library."
    "A product of the ERIC Clearinghouse on Handicapped and Gifted
Children."
    Includes bibliographical references (p.).
    ISBN 0-86586-204-4
    1. Handicapped youth—Vocational education—United States.
2. Vocational guidance for the handicapped—United States.
3. Social skills—Study and teaching (Secondary)—United States.
I. Gaylord-Ross, Robert.   II. Council for Exceptional Children.
III. ERIC Clearinghouse on Handicapped and Gifted Children.
IV. Title.   V. Series.
LC4019.7.B85   1991
371.93—dc20   91-3029
                                                                      CIP

ISBN 0-86586-204-4

A product of the ERIC Clearinghouse on Handicapped and Gifted Children

Published in 1991 by The Council for Exceptional Children, 1920 Association
Drive, Reston, Virginia 22091-1589.
Stock No. P345

This publication was prepared with funding from the U.S. Department of
Education, Office of Educational Research and Improvement, contract no.
RI88062007. Contractors undertaking such projects under government sponsor-
ship are encouraged to express freely their judgment in professional and
technical matters. Prior to publication the manuscript was submitted for critical
review and determination of professional competence. This publication has met
such standards. Points of view, however, do not necessarily represent the
official view or opinions of either The Council for Exceptional Children or the
Department of Education.

Printed in the United States of America
10 9 8 7 6 5 4 3 2 1

Contents

Foreword

Working with Behavioral Disorders
CEC Mini-Library

One of the greatest underserved populations in the schools today is students who have severe emotional and behavioral problems. These students present classroom teachers and other school personnel with the challenges of involving them effectively in the learning process and facilitating their social and emotional development.

The editors have coordinated a series of publications that address a number of critical issues facing service providers in planning and implementing more appropriate programs for children and youth with severe emotional and behavioral problems. There are nine booklets in this Mini-Library series, each one designed for a specific purpose.

- *Teaching Students with Behavioral Disorders: Basic Questions and Answers* addresses questions that classroom teachers commonly ask about instructional issues, classroom management, teacher collaboration, and assessment and identification of students with emotional and behavioral disorders.

- *Conduct Disorders and Social Maladjustments: Policies, Politics, and Programming* examines the issues associated with providing services to students who exhibit externalizing or acting-out behaviors in the schools.

- *Behaviorally Disordered? Assessment for Identification and Instruction* discusses systematic screening procedures and the need for functional assessment procedures that will facilitate provision of services to students with emotional and behavioral disorders.

- *Preparing to Integrate Students with Behavioral Disorders* provides guidelines to assist in the integration of students into mainstream settings and the delivery of appropriate instructional services to these students.

- *Teaching Young Children with Behavioral Disorders* highlights the applications of Public Law 99–457 for young children with special needs and delineates a variety of interventions that focus on both young children and their families.

- *Reducing Undesirable Behaviors* provides procedures to reduce undesirable behavior in the schools and lists specific recommendations for using these procedures.

- *Social Skills for Students with Autism* presents information on using a variety of effective strategies for teaching social skills to children and youth with autism.

- *Special Education in Juvenile Corrections* highlights the fact that a large percentage of youth incarcerated in juvenile correctional facilities has special learning, social, and emotional needs. Numerous practical suggestions are delineated for providing meaningful special education services in these settings.

- *Moving On: Transitions for Youth with Behavioral Disorders* presents practical approaches to working with students in vocational settings and provides examples of successful programs and activities.

We believe that this Mini-Library series will be of great benefit to those endeavoring to develop new programs or enhance existing programs for students with emotional and behavioral disorders.

Lyndal M. Bullock
Robert B. Rutherford, Jr.

Preface

Youth with behavioral disorders present a great challenge to vocational education and transition programming. It is one thing to teach a student a few job tasks in an isolated setting; it is quite another to teach the person to display a myriad of critical behaviors in a "real" work setting in order to hold a job.

Vocational education for persons with behavioral disorders is a relatively new, yet growing field; and an instructional technology is emerging to fulfill the goals of the transition initiative. In this book, we suggest an ecological and curricular approach to vocational assessment and training. Here, the individual is portrayed within a political and educational context. Vocational education cannot rely on educators alone; it must also get substantive support from the business world in hiring and funding programs for people with disabilities. These programs must rely on the highest level of behavioral technology to manage and suppress disruptive behaviors in the workplace as well as teach prosocial skills.

Because of the presence of antisocial behaviors and the absence of positive social skills, the typical student with behavioral disorders is a poor candidate for job placement and retention. Yet, social competence at work can be engendered through interventions that foster social skills and develop supportive social relationships. The analysis of social support networks and, particularly, benefactor roles in the workplace, hold great promise for enhancing the employability and community integration of these students.

In Memory

When we began this monograph back in the fall of 1989, I had no idea that my last writing on it would be this memorial to Robert Gaylord-Ross's life and his untimely death. I still have a hard time believing that anything could harm Robert. He was a man who exuded infectious energy and a silent sense of physical and mental strength. When I first heard the news that Robert had died of a cerebral hemorrhage on December 19, 1990, I was sure that some terrible mistake had been made—that it was another person with the same name or I had heard the voice on the end of the phone incorrectly. But there had been no error; my dear friend and colleague was dead at the age of 45.

Robert's career in the special education and rehabilitation field spanned some 17 years as a psychologist, researcher, and professor. In that time he was incredibly productive, securing over $3 million of grant funds and publishing over 100 articles, chapters, and books. It is an overused phrase in our field, but his work on the social integration of persons with disabilities in school, vocational, and community settings was truly "at the cutting edge." It served as a standard that waved in the breeze and showed the rest of us how these kinds of projects should be done. What most impressed me was that he was very learned and respected in so many different areas including severe disabilities, autism, learning disabilities, and—as this manuscript attests—behavior disorders. He also produced and befriended numerous new doctoral level people, offering opportunities to these Ph.D.s that would shape and foster their careers. There is a great hole in our field where Robert stood, and I fear that his place will not soon be filled.

It is unfair, though, to view his life solely in terms of work, as Robert was much more than an academic. He was always fun to speak with; it didn't take too much to launch him into his passion, basketball, or to talk about the true love of his life, his family—Cory, Alexa, and Asher. It seems unfair that he was taken from them at such a young age. I pray that their grief will be softened, at least somewhat, by memories of him and the knowledge that he thought the world of each of them.

In one of my last conversations with Robert, he asked me about my own family, and after I answered he replied, "Well, give them a hug for me and hold them close, because you just never know what can happen." No, buddy, you never do—adios and thanks for everything.

Michael Bullis
Winter, 1991

Introduction

There is perhaps no disability group as misunderstood and as under-served as youth with behavioral disorders (BD). Moreover, there is an absence of research and development specific to the community integration and vocational training of this population. Nelson and Kauffman (1977) found that "the provision of educational services for behaviorally disturbed adolescents has lagged far behind services for younger pupils, particularly in the public schools" (p. 102) and that there is a dearth of curricular materials for use with these students. Scruggs and Mastropieri (1985), in a review of all articles published in the *Journal of Behavioral Disorders*, noted few studies on youth and virtually no research conducted with this group in vocational or community settings. The lack of an empirical foundation for vocational and functional life skills interventions is further underscored in three monographs (Braaten, Rutherford, & Evans, 1985; Braaten, Rutherford, & Kardash, 1985; Fink & Kokasha, 1983), in which service programs and research designed specifically for adolescents with behavioral disorders are presented. Each reference acknowledges that relatively few programs have been developed for this clientele and that very little research has been conducted on these issues.

In recent years, projects have been initiated to examine the postschool work experiences of students with disabilities. Some projects have included youth with BD (e.g., Hasazi, Gordon, & Roe, 1985; Mithaug, Horiuchi, & Fanning, 1985); and isolated vocational demonstration projects have been conducted with this population (e.g., Gaylord-Ross, 1986; Nishioka-Evans, 1987). From these efforts, the following is known:

1. Many students with BD drop out of school before completion (Butler-Nalin & Padilla, 1989; Edgar & Levine, 1987; Wagner & Shaver, 1989).

2. Most do not go on to postsecondary education programs (Neel, Meadows, Levine, & Edgar, 1988).

3. High rates of unemployment are encountered (Hasazi et al., 1985).

4. If work is secured, the jobs that are obtained tend to be menial in nature with a limited future (Neel et al., 1988).

5. Many vocational problems experienced by workers with BD relate to inappropriate social behavior in the workplace (Bullis, Nishioka-Evans, & Fredericks, 1990; Gaylord-Ross, Siegel, & Bullis, 1990).

One answer to these problems is to provide these youth with comprehensive vocational and functional skill training while in school, in the hope that they will succeed in their vocational and community integration endeavors after leaving that setting. However, there is little research in this area, and few concrete rules exist to structure such programs. This absence of information is crucial to professionals charged with providing vocational and functional skill training. These students can be challenging enough to serve within the confines of the school building. When programs are extended to the unique and usually less structured environment of community-based sites, the service delivery issues compound in complexity, and the possibilities for trouble multiply. Moreover, the youth's transition from the school environment to the community can often be complicated by a lack of adult service resources and confusion in the service delivery process (Kortering & Edgar, 1988; Maddox & Edgar, 1988).

The purpose of this monograph is to review and discuss the existing literature on this topic. First, we summarize research that has been conducted on the transition experiences and community adjustment of youth with behavioral disorders. Second, we examine assessment procedures that can be used to structure vocational instruction. Third, we present social skill training procedures specific to vocational preparation and placements for this group. Fourth, we offer overviews of two model demonstration vocational training programs. Finally, we discuss the business, societal, and political factors that affect both the general job market and the employment opportunities for these students.

At the outset, we should note that the population of students with BD should not be considered as homogeneous. It is well established that two broad-band dimensions of deviant behavior are exhibited by these children and youth (Achenbach, 1966; 1985):

The "broad-band" grouping designated as Internalizing mainly involves problems within the self, such as unhappiness and fears. The broad-band grouping designated by Externalizing, by contrast, mainly involves conflicts with others, such as aggressive, delinquent, and overactive behavior. (Achenbach & McConaughy, 1987, p. 33)

Unfortunately, students with BD often are considered as being similar, or at least are presented as such in research and program descriptions. This approach obscures important intersubject differences, making it difficult—if not impossible—to develop potent curricula and service programs for students' unique characteristics and needs (Mac-Millan & Morrison, 1979; MacMillan & Kavale, 1986). Further, the results of these investigations are difficult to generalize or understand because the parameters of the samples are seldom specified in great enough detail to draw inferences about the type of student for whom a particular intervention is effective (Kavale, Forness, & Alper, 1986). As efforts are directed at the development and evaluation of work-related interventions for the broad population of students with BD, it will be critical to address the unique needs of subgroups of adolescents to construct the best services possible and to verify for whom interventions are effective or ineffective.

The reader is advised that the current literature and research base is not clearly divided according to this behavioral dichotomy. The research reported here indicates that students with behavioral disorders often are grouped and treated similarly in intervention and data analysis. The exception to this practice is with work conducted with youth with externalizing behavior—those displaying aggressive, conduct disordered, or delinquent behavior. Thus, the findings of some studies may have limited applicability to certain groups of students (e.g., results from a study on delinquent youth may not be relevant to youth who exhibit extreme withdrawal and depression).

1. Long-Term Life Adjustment

Research shows that almost all adults with adjustment problems had behavioral problems as children. Having a behavioral problem in childhood, however, does not guarantee antisocial behavior in later life.

Individual development is ultimately validated by long-term life adjustment. Moreover, the success (or lack of it) achieved by students in their transition from the school to the community can serve as an index of program effectiveness and the basis on which to revise interventions to address critical student needs. It is then crucial that a solid knowledge base be established on the community experiences of youth with behavioral disorders. This knowledge base can drive program change and individual service provision.

Will's original concept of transition and the goal of transition for all students with disabilities emphasizes employment:

> Employment represents an important outcome of education and transition for all Americans. The goal of OSERS [Office of Special Education and Rehabilitation Services] programming for transition is that individuals leaving the school system obtain jobs, whether immediately after school or after a period of post-secondary education or vocational services. Employment is a critical aspect of the lives of most adults in our society, whether their work involves highly paid career specializations, entry level jobs, or working in situations where ongoing support services are provided. Paid employment offers opportunities to expand social contacts, contribute to society, demonstrate creativity, and establish an adult identity. The income generated by work creates purchasing power in the community, makes community integration easier, expands the range of available choices, enhances independence, and creates personal status. Of course, this concern with employment does not indicate a lack of interest in other aspects of adult living. Success in social, personal, leisure, and other adult roles enhances opportunities both to obtain employment and to enjoy its benefits. (Will, 1984, p. 4)

On the other hand, the emphasis given to employment in the transition effort has been questioned (Edgar, 1987, 1988; Halpern, 1985). Halpern discussed the need to conceptualize transition in terms of community integration instead of only employment:

> Two examples, one from common sense and the other from legislation, may help to illustrate the point. Consider the person who has a job, but constantly gets into debt over his head, fails to pay his bills on time, and does such a poor job of maintaining his apartment that the landlord resorts to eviction. Good vocational skills will not solve these problems, and vocational training would not be the correct way to address these problems. Other services with other objectives are required. Recent legislation has also supported the concept of different needs being addressed by different programs and services. For example, the 1978 amendments to the Rehabilitation Act authorized independent living as a legitimate agency goal to be addressed by a separate service delivery system

under the auspices of the vocational rehabilitation program. (Halpern, 1985, p. 482)

It makes sense to us that transition should be considered in terms of assessing quality of life—a broad life- and community-adjustment perspective encompassing social networks, community participation, and employment. In addition, for youth with behavioral disorders, salient markers of pathology (emotional crises, incarceration, and hospitalization) demand attention. It is beyond the purview of this monograph to review the voluminous literature reviewing predictive relationships between child characteristics, experiences, and programs, and the long-term adult adjustment of people with behavioral and emotional disorders (Kazdin, 1987a, 1987b; Parker & Asher, 1987; Robins, 1978); yet it is useful to examine some of the salient features of this literature. The few studies that present employment and transition data for youth with behavioral disorders are discussed in this section.

The following investigations illustrate the kinds of studies that describe the complex relationships between child and adult psychopathology. Though this review is by no means exhaustive of the literature, the findings provide a foundation to foster a basic understanding of the adult adjustment of these students. It should be cautioned that the bulk of these studies focuses on persons with externalizing problems and on males. There has been little research conducted on females, although there is some indication that they are receiving increased attention (Gaffney & McFall, 1981; Henggeler, 1989).

A now-classic study by Cowen, Pederson, Babijian, Izzo, and Troust (1973) pointed to the substantial relationship between child and adult maladjustment. Almost all of the adults with adjustment problems had problems as children. Yet, the corresponding relationship does not hold when looking forward from childhood to adulthood. That is, just because a child displays antisocial behavior does not guarantee that he or she will display antisocial behavior in later life. Robins (1978, 1979), summarizing the frequently cited studies that she and her colleagues conducted, suggests that most antisocial children do *not* become antisocial adults, even though adult maladjustment virtually requires childhood maladjustment. Further, she states that evidence of a variety of antisocial behavior in childhood is predictive of adult antisocial behavior, and that the prediction of adult antisocial behavior is not influenced greatly by socioeconomic status.

In a similar vein, Olweus (1977) investigated two samples of boys over a period of 1 and 3 years, respectively, in which the subjects' antisocial behaviors were rated on a regular basis by peer raters and then related to external criteria of teacher ratings and nominations of antisocial behavior. Correlations of the data across time revealed a relatively stable pattern of aggressive social behavior. Olweus (1979) also examined a series of studies on the stability of antisocial behavior in boys and found moderate correlations across childhood and adolescent behavior patterns. Loeber (1982), in another review of the literature, concluded that there is "support to the notion that youths whose early antisocial behavior is extremely frequent are at highest risk for becoming chronic offenders. Moreover, there is good evidence that youngsters who turn out to become chronic offenders start their antisocial behavior at an early age" (p. 1442). Interestingly, Loeber also found that the type of antisocial behavior engaged in by youth tends to change from preadolescence to adolescence, with the number of persons who engage in overt acts declining and the number of youth who engage in covert acts increasing. Other research supports the fact that early aggression is highly predictive of delinquency (Roff & Wirt, 1984) and adult maladjustment in terms of criminality, spouse abuse, traffic violations, and physical aggression (Huesmann, Eron, Lefkowitz, & Walder, 1984; Mitchell & Rosa, 1981).

Some data have suggested that specific types of deviant behavior vary in stability and that antisocial behaviors vary in the way in which they are exhibited. For example, sexual offenses appear highly resistant to intervention and tend to be displayed in an enduring pattern (Davis & Leitenberg, 1987). Conversely, boys who are hyperactive, but who do not exhibit conduct disorders, are much more likely to outgrow the condition, as compared to hyperactive boys who also exhibit conduct disorders (August, Stewart, & Holmes, 1983). Loeber and Schmaling (1985a) conducted a meta-analysis of research findings to confirm that there is ample evidence to support the notion that antisocial behavior among male youth can empirically be considered in terms of three forms: covert (stealing), overt (fighting), and versatile (displaying both covert and overt social behaviors). Loeber and Schmaling (1985b) also found that "versatile" antisocial youth scored higher across a number of measures of antisocial behaviors than did students considered as "pure" overt or covert offenders.

Comprehensive reviews of extensive numbers of studies conducted by Gerald Patterson and his colleagues at the Oregon Social Learning Center (Reid, 1989) and epidemiological investigations (Farrington, 1986; Loeber & Dishion, 1983) support the position that a child's socioeconomic status is not, in and of itself, causally related to adult antisocial behavior. Instead, it is clear that there is a strong and primary relationship between maladaptive child rearing and a dysfunctional family environment with the individual's maladjustment in adult life.

Finally, many studies have indicated that behavioral disturbances during the adolescent and adult years are related to social skill deficits (Dishion, Loeber, Stouthamer-Loeber, & Patterson, 1984; Freedman, Donahoe, Rosenthal, Schlundt, & McFall, 1978; Gaffney & McFall, 1981; Hazel, Schumaker, Sherman, & Sheldon-Wildgen, 1982), social cognition (Dodge, 1980), and deficits in social problem-solving thinking (Chandler,

1973; Kendall, Deardorff, & Finch, 1977; Levinson & Neuringer, 1971; Platt, Scura, & Hannon, 1973; Platt, Spivack, Altman, & Altman, 1974; Slaby & Guerra, 1988). Janes, Hesselbrock, Myers, and Penniman (1979) found a single teacher-related item, "Fails to get along with other children," was closely related to a variety of adult antisocial behaviors. In a comprehensive review of the literature, Parker and Asher (1987) found "general support for the hypothesis that children with poor peer adjustment are at risk for later life difficulties" (p. 357). The support was clearest for low acceptance and aggressiveness as predictors of dropping out of school and criminality. Parker and Asher also commented on the relationship of poor peer adjustment and occupational success.

> It is not difficult to imagine that children who have problems getting along with classmates might later have problems getting along with co-workers and supervisors. Thus, we might expect low-accepted children to fare relatively poorly in later interviews for jobs, to be less satisfied with their jobs, and to evidence poorer performance and attendance records. (Parker & Asher, 1987, p. 382)

In summary, not all externalizing adolescents will exhibit long-term aggressive and antisocial behavior, but it is clear that this general behavior pattern is enduring and relatively stable. The fact that the kinds of deviant behaviors engaged in by this group tend to change over time is important and carries implications for treatment and prevention. Available data also suggest that the family environment and social skills are central to adult adjustment and that social competence is related to employment tenure and success.

2. Transition Studies

Youth with behavioral disorders experience a high dropout rate; as a result, many of these students never have access to training designed to prepare them for meaningful careers.

An important question is, What happens to youth with behavioral disorders after they leave school? Unfortunately, very few follow-up studies have tracked these persons and documented their experiences in the community. In a recent investigation, Neel et al. (1988) surveyed a cohort of youth with behavioral disorders who had graduated from schools in the state of Washington. Neel et al. collected employment and continuing education data on 160 young adults whom they were able to contact. At the time of data collection, 60% of the youth were employed and 78% of these had been employed at some time since leaving school. Of the group sampled, 17% were attending some form of postsecondary education, a total of 31% were unengaged (not working or attending school), and 58% were living at home.

Neel et al. (1988) contrasted their findings for the group with BD with norms they established with a comparable large sample cohort of youth without disabilities in Washington. The latter group achieved a current employment rate of 70%, and 85% had been employed at some time since leaving high school. A total of 47% were in postsecondary education, and only 8% were unengaged. Sixty-six percent of the sample were living at home. Thus, the youth with behavioral disorders were employed at a rate 10% less than the group without disabilities and were involved in postsecondary education at a much lower rate. Because of the educational variable, there was a much higher proportion of "un-engagement" of the group with behavioral disorders. The Neel et al. study is important as it presents norms on important variables while permitting contrasts with a normative group.

However, it must be noted that the persons with behavioral disorders in this study had graduated from high school. Although the dropout rates of students with disabilities have only recently been established, it is a general assumption that this group has one of—if not *the*—highest rates of leaving school before successful completion. Current studies (Butler-Nalin & Padilla, 1989; Wagner & Shaver, 1989) have provided information on the dropout rates of all categories of students served under the special education umbrella. In this nationally based and rep-resentative study, students with BD experienced a dropout rate of 54.7%. Not only was this finding higher than that experienced by other dis-ability groups, it is also more than double the generally agreed-on 20% to 25% dropout rate for all students (disabled and nondisabled). Thus, Neel et al.'s sample, consisting only of graduates, is probably unrepresen-tative of the population at large and suggests a higher level of functioning than actually exists. Moreover, high dropout rates indicate that many BD students never access, much less complete, postsecondary training designed to prepare them for meaningful careers.

The National Longitudinal Transition Study (NLTS) (Wagner & Shaver, 1989) has collected data on youth with disabilities in transition and presents data that confirms this point. In this study, for the cohort of students with behavioral disorders who were 1 year out of school (and who left school through a variety of avenues, e.g., graduate, drop out), only 50% of the youths were employed, a figure 10% below that reported by Neel et al. (1988).

Two frequently cited studies conducted by Hasazi et al. (1985) in Vermont and Mithaug et al. (1985) in Colorado include youth with behavioral disorders, but specific data for this group are not reported. In general, though, it appears that the subjects in these studies tended to find jobs on their own, did not use adult service agencies, and if employed found jobs that paid a low wage. The youth believed that special education prepared them to work in the community, but that more training in social participation in the community and job search methods would have been helpful in their school-to-community transition. Hasazi et al. (1985) found that participation in paid employment while in high school was correlated to successful employment after leaving high school in a statistically significant way.

In one of the few studies focusing solely on the vocational adjustment of adolescents with behavioral disorders, Cook, Solomon, and Mock (1988) followed 30 youth who had been placed in competitive jobs as part of a supported work project. It was found that, on the average, subjects in this group held their first jobs for 125 days and then moved to a second job that they held for 109 days. These job changes were not necessarily to move to better positions, but rather related to boredom or the urge to experience another type of work. Interestingly, those youth identified as schizophrenic were more stable on their jobs and considered better workers than those students considered as acting out or aggressive, because the behaviors of this latter group of students do not match the demands of the work setting.

Follow-up data collected from The Career Ladder Program (CLP) have relevance to students with BD (this program is described in detail in a later section). Although the program primarily served a population with learning disabilities, about 10% of the 100 graduates had serious behavioral disturbances. Siegel, Greener, Prieur, and Gaylord-Ross (1989) asked graduates of this vocational training program to provide retrospective data on their lives at 6-month intervals after graduation. They found that the group leveled off at an 80% rate of employment. About 27% of the group attended postsecondary education, and only 7% were unengaged. The CLP attempted to place its students in upwardly mobile positions, rather than entry-level, dead-end positions. In this regard, the CLP participants reported many more positive than negative changes in their jobs. Financially, the CLP youth averaged $5.80 per hour in their jobs. This compared favorably with the NLTS wage of $4.30 per hour for youth with learning disabilities (Wagner & Shaver, 1989). Siegel et al. (1989) make an argument for a safety net of vocational services for youth with mild disabilities. That is, they infer that the superior employment statistics for the CLP participants resulted from the ongoing vocational support services provided from 10th grade through the postsecondary years. Thus, the CLP data usefully provide wage and longitudinal data for a group of students similar to youth with BD and support the case that such a program could be applied to these students.

Isolated studies have suggested that vocational interventions foster positive psychological adjustment on psychometric measures shortly after treatment (Massimo & Shore, 1963) and at 10 months posttreatment (Shore, Massimo, & Mack, 1965). Further, there is some evidence that vocational preparation may influence "at risk" students to complete school. Thornton and Zigmond (1987a, 1987b, 1988) found consistent correlation between high school completion and vocational education among groups of students with learning disabilities. In a review of the regular vocational education literature, Bishop (1989) stated that appropriate vocational training can have a strong influence on at-risk students' school completion and ultimate occupational success.

Another transition subject to receive attention relates to the network between schools and community-based agencies (e.g., vocational rehabilitation) serving students with BD. In an examination of the transition experiences of all students with disabilities who left 15 school districts in Washington between 1976 and 1984, Kortering and Edgar (1988) examined a sample of 121 adolescents and young adults with behavioral disorders. Kortering and Edgar found that only 5% of this sample had any contact with vocational rehabilitation, approximately 50% were unemployed, and of those employed the majority found their jobs on their own or through a friend or family member. Other studies from Washington, Maddox and Webb (1986) and Maddox and Edgar (1988), found significant problems in the transition of students in juvenile correctional institutions to home, schools, and with human service agencies. In general, these problems related to a lack of awareness of the functions and responsibilities among involved parties. Maddox and Edgar identified seven key issues that should be dealt with to effect a positive transition experience: program awareness, eligibility and program entrance requirements, exchange of information and communication, program planning before transition, feedback and follow-up after transition, written procedures, and parent involvement. Maddox and Webb implemented a transition planning program with selected sites and programs in Washington and found that systematic procedures structured to address these issues did, in fact, improve the transfer of students from correctional agencies to public schools.

3. Vocational Assessment

A vocational assessment should provide information about a student's physical, emotional, and intellectual capabilities; determine the student's knowledge and awareness of work; test performances in various controlled settings; and observe the student's behavior in a "real" job placement.

Given the poor community adjustment experiences of youth with BD, it is clear that the vocational training afforded these people must be focused, addressing key weaknesses to be of maximum benefit. Consequently, vocational programs must be guided by and based on clear and accurate assessment information. Simply, data of this type should identify the student's work-related strengths and weaknesses and provide a foundation for instruction, monitoring of learning, and a guide to job placements. This section begins with a description of "traditional" vocational evaluation. Next, we present a theoretical model of work requirements and behaviors. Third, we present guidelines for conducting comprehensive vocational assessments of students with behavioral disorders in school-based vocational training programs.

Traditional Vocational Evaluation

Vocational evaluation (Pruitt, 1976) has its roots within the rehabilitation field. The following is a definition of vocational evaluation:

> A comprehensive process that systematically uses work, real or simulated, as the focal point for assessment and vocational exploration, the purpose of which is to assist individuals in vocational development. Vocational evaluation incorporates medical, psychological, social, vocational, educational, cultural, and economic data in the attainment of the goals of the evaluation process. (Vocational Evaluation and Work Adjustment Association, 1975, p. 86)

The primary objective of traditional vocational evaluation procedures is to match an individual with a specific job or to recommend that the person enter training for a particular career. This type of evaluation is typically implemented within a rehabilitation facility or vocational evaluation center during a specific period of time (e.g., 4 to 6 weeks). This focus and technique is understandable, as rehabilitation has historically been concerned with adults, who may have vocational experience and the wherewithal to make informed career decisions or to be placed in a specific job or job path.

The type of assessment tool that is most often paired with vocational evaluation is the commercially available work sample (e.g., Singer Vocational Evaluation System, McCarron-Dial Work Evaluation System, the Tower system), or locally developed work samples that are developed to represent jobs available in communities. Essentially, these instruments represent facsimiles or analog interpretations of work environments and their demands (Vocational Evaluation and Work Adjustment Association, 1975). For example, a cubicle with a particular type of job (welding) may compose part of a work sample system. The person being assessed is asked to work at the sample while his or her performance is monitored. In some instances, these exercises may be completed in a few hours, and in other cases the exercise may run for more than a day. In addition, the process will also use multiple assessment instruments and procedures (psychometric tests, aptitude and achievement tests, vocational interest inventories, and situational assessments).

However, the "traditional" approach is not suitable to the instructional needs of school-based vocational programs and the developmental nature of students' learning in these programs. The primary goal of vocational instruction is to promote the growth and development of the student over time. As students are likely to, and undoubtedly will, develop work skills and expand their vocational horizons as the result of exposure to various work experiences, they do not constitute a fully formed "product" whose characteristics and potential can be measured through one static assessment procedure. It follows that traditional vocational evaluation, focusing on the individual at one point in time, will be inappropriate to reflect the student's growth from learning, nor will such data have utility for measuring the direction and structure of the vocational education intervention over time (Cobb, 1983; Cobb & Lakin, 1985). In line with this point, Sitlington, Brolin, Clark, and Vacanti (1985), in the position statement of the Council for Exceptional Children's Division on Career Development on career/vocational assessment, stated:

> The goals of this process should be specifically geared to providing the information needed to make decisions in all areas of career programming; these decisions may be related to developing an individualized program (curriculum content) for the handicapped learner or determining what assistance the learner needs to succeed in an ongoing program. (p. 4)

Additionally, attention must be given to the standardization and psychometric properties of the instruments used in the vocational assessment effort. There has been little empirical work directed to the development and standardization of vocational assessment instruments for students with behavioral disorders; thus, tools used in this type of evaluation may lack desired item statistics, reliability, and validity (De-Stefano, 1987).

Finally, caution should be exercised over the relevance of data from psychometric tests to the vocational education of students with behavioral disorders. Questions have been raised about the utility and applicability of these instruments in measuring the vocational capacities and skills of people with disabilities (Frey, 1984). Although such discussion has not been applied specifically to persons with behavioral disorders, B. Cohen and Anthony (1984) have examined the relationship of psychometric data (i.e., intelligence and personality test results) to the rehabilitation outcomes of adults with various psychiatric diagnoses. These researchers found that this type of information was not related to vocational attainment or rehabilitation success, and they argued that the assessment effort should focus on subjects' functional skills instead of abstract psychometric constructs.

It may be concluded that school-based vocational assessment for students with behavioral disorders should *not* be structured along the lines of traditional vocational evaluation procedures (Hursh & Kerns, 1988). The question then becomes, How should such programs be designed?

Theoretical Model

Numerous authors (Cobb & Lakin, 1985; Ianacone & Leconte, 1986; Porter & Stodden, 1986; Stodden, Ianacone, Boone, & Bisconer, 1987) suggest that the most appropriate vocational assessment procedures for students in school settings are informal methods that mirror curriculum demands at key decision points. Of course, if assessment is tied to the vocational curriculum, it is mandatory that the crucial content to be taught in the vocational program can be identified (Chadsey-Rusch, 1986; Foss, Walker, Todis, Lyman, & Smith, 1986).

To prepare students for successful employment, interventions should be structured to address four broad domains: the worker's vocational interests and needs, task performance, work adjustment, and social/interpersonal behavior on the job. First, to match the individual with a job that she or he will enjoy and be successful at, it is necessary to analyze the student's vocational interests and requirements for what will be gained from the job (Loftquist & Dawis, 1969).

Second, to succeed in the employment arena the individual must be able to perform the required job tasks in a satisfactory manner. Such performance can be considered in terms of the student's physical and cognitive abilities, general work skills, and specific job skills. Essentially, the person's physical and cognitive abilities are the foundation of his or her work potential and, in some way, dictate the kind of work in which he or she may be involved. General work skills refer to competencies that may be required in numerous jobs and constitute task clusters (e.g., the ability to type, to use tools, etc.). To be successful on a specific job, a worker must be able to exhibit the necessary prerequisite skills for that particular job.

Third, work adjustment is composed of the formal and informal work rules that dictate how an employment setting operates. These skills are peripherally associated with the production requirements of the job and conform to fundamental notions of how an employee should present himself or herself at work. Aspects of work adjustment include appropriate dress and grooming for the specific job, exhibiting enthusiasm and motivation to work, following safety regulations on the job, being punctual in coming to work and having regular attendance, and demonstrating sufficient attention to the job task.

Fourth, several studies provide evidence that the primary correlate of success or lack of success of workers with behavioral disorders in job placements relates to their level of social/interpersonal competence in the employment setting, that is, the ability to "get along" with others on the job (Anthony, 1979; Dellario, Goldfield, Farkas, & Cohen, 1984; Griffiths, 1973, 1974; Hursh, 1983; Watts, 1978). Reviews of the literature on social competence in employment for workers with disabilities by Chadsey-Rusch (1986), Foss et al. (1986), and Salzberg, Lignugaris/Kraft, and McCuller (1988) specify three general categories of job-related social behavior: disruptive behavior, supervisor relations, and co-worker relations.

Disruptive behavior refers to bizarre, emotional behavior that may be either aggressive or extremely withdrawn. It also includes stealing and sexually deviant behavior. These kinds of behaviors may have a long-standing history or be associated with transient stress or specific environmental stimuli.

Supervisor relations are ways in which the worker interacts with the work supervisor. Content areas include the ability to respond appropriately to criticism or correction, being able to request information or assistance to complete a work task, being able to follow work-related instructions, and being able to ask for time off or quit a job.

Co-worker relations are ways in which the worker interacts with other workers in the employment setting. Three content areas have been identified: exhibiting cooperative work behavior, being able to handle teasing or provoking from other workers, and being able to resolve personal concerns. Foss et al. (1986) also emphasized the importance of relationship-building skills, that is, the ability to develop friendships and supportive relationships with co-workers.

Unfortunately, these descriptions are too broad to be helpful in specifying the exact kinds of social problems experienced by adolescents and young adults with behavioral disorders in work placements. Unless we know what specific problems to address when teaching these students how to behave on the job, we may not focus on issues that are, in fact, encountered or important (Freedman et al., 1978; Gaffney & McFall, 1981; McFall, 1982; Romano & Bellack, 1980; Strain, 1982).

One project with such a focus is being conducted by the first author of this monograph and his colleagues (Bullis & Fredericks, 1988). The primary intent of the project is to develop measures of job-related social behavior for youth with behavioral disorders. The major emphasis of the initial part of this research effort has been to identify and describe the specific social problems experienced in the workplace by members of this population. Toward this end, the project is using the Behavioral-Analytic Model of test development (Goldfried & D'Zurilla, 1969). This technique requires that social problems be examined in the context in which they occur (i.e., the work setting), and to involve members of the target population (i.e., adolescents with behavioral disorders) and significant others (i.e., work trainers and employers) in the specification of test content.

To gain such information, interviews were conducted with youth, employers, and work trainers around 16 major job-related social content areas culled from the available literature (accepting criticism or correction from a work supervisor; requesting help from a work supervisor; following instructions from a work supervisor; quitting a job; taking time off; working as fast as co-worker; talking to a work supervisor about a problem; working with a co-worker to complete a job; dealing with teasing or provoking from co-workers; personal concerns; making friends with co-workers; talking with a co-worker about his or her behavior; being talked to by a co-worker about a problem; fighting; stealing and lying; and dating). The questions across interview forms were worded differently for each audience, and all responses were recorded by the interviewer in the form of a short vignette. The interviews took roughly 45 to 80 minutes each to complete.

A total of 58 adolescents with competitive work experience, 11 work trainers, and 12 employers and co-workers was interviewed. The number of social problems generated under the questions ranged in frequency across questions from 31 to 117, with a total of over 1,100 social problems generated across all 16 areas of questioning. Examples of several representative social problem vignettes that were generated are shown in Figure 1.

Next, this initial list of problems was reviewed and edited to create a representative sampling of 237 social problems youth with behavioral disorders experience in job settings. During the rest of the project, those specific problems that are both important and prevalent in work settings will be identified through a national survey of service providers. Research also will be conducted to identify the kinds of responses youth

FIGURE 1
Examples of Specific Job-related Social Problems

- Grant was hired to be a mechanic in an automobile repair shop, but all he was allowed to do was clean up. He went in to work on his birthday, hoping that on that day he would be allowed to do mechanical work. He was very disappointed when he realized he was to do clean-up again.

- Tina worked with a co-worker who continually made fun of her and called her names. Tina tried to ignore the girl, but finally had enough and asked her to please stop. The co-worker laughed and said "I won't stop, your're too much fun to give s _ _ _ to."

- John worked on an assembly line with his boss. The boss was unable to finish a task, so John leaned over and did it for him, saying, "A f _ _ _ _ _ _ idiot could do that right."

- Mike completed an assignment at work and thought he had done it correctly. The boss checked his work and told Mike that there were many mistakes and he would have to do the job all over again. Mike became frustrated and wanted to quit the job.

- Michelle got a new job as a waitress. After Michelle arrived at work on Friday night the boss told her that she would have to stay and close up the restaurant. Michelle didn't want to stay because she had a date, but her boss was very insistent she stay late.

- Sally was working on an assembly job. While she was bending over a male co-worker grabbed her hair to get her attention. This surprised Sally and made her mad.

could make when faced with these problems, to identify the most correct response to each problem from the perspective of competitive employers, and to integrate this information into the assessment instruments.

Knowing how to act or respond in a certain situation is most probably a necessary prerequisite to performing the correct behavior. It is, however, entirely possible that a person may know what to do in a situation, but for some reason not perform in an appropriate manner. Consequently, vocational assessment of job-related social behavior should include both knowledge-based and performance-based instruments (Bullis & Foss, 1986; Gresham, 1986; Kendall & Braswell, 1982; McFall, 1982). At this point, it is anticipated that one of the assessment tools will be designed to measure a subject's knowledge of social skills in the workplace through an individual, clinical interview. A second measure will be constructed for use by service providers to rate student's actual social performance while at work. Ultimately, these measures could be used within an assessment approach such as that presented in the next section.

Assessment Guidelines

Vocational assessment should be considered as a longitudinal, developmental process and conceptualized in terms of four progressive categories. First, it is important to gather data for basic screening purposes to analyze students' physical, emotional, and intellectual capabilities and to establish a rough gauge of his or her work potential. Second, it is necessary to assess the student's knowledge and awareness of work as a starting point in the instructional process. Both of these first two phases may use psychometric measures, achievement tests, and paper-and-pencil tests of functional skills (e.g., work adjustment skills) to gain perspective on the individual's basic skills. In most cases, the purpose of the assessments should be to establish (a) instructional guidelines on generic job skills and (b) baseline information on the student's raw and untested job potential.

Third, the student should initially, but only as the beginning step in the vocational training process, be placed on various analog work sites (e.g., commercially and locally developed work samples) and sheltered job sites (e.g., make-work in school or classroom settings) to analyze basic job capabilities and potential, foster multiple work skills, expand work interests, and promote the generalization of these skills to different environments (e.g., accepting criticism and correction from more than one supervisor). Fourth, it is *absolutely critical* that students be placed in competitive or quasi-competitive jobs in the community as soon as ready, to foster vocational development and to gain an accurate picture of what his or her *real* job skills are in actual work settings under those pressures and conditions. All of these phases should emphasize performance data derived from ratings and behavioral observation. These data should be used to shape eventual job placement and continuing education decisions made by the student and the work-experience coordinator.

In line with this approach, several general guidelines should be followed.

1. Any vocational assessment must examine not only the individual but also the vocational environment. These efforts must focus on the kinds of jobs that are available and their respective demands (e.g., what one has to do to explain the job) and rewards (e.g., pay). In addition, a "tolerance" factor among employers seems to be

critical in job placement. That is, some employers are more apt to accept employee differences or are more willing to work to accommodate the shortcomings of some workers. At present, we do not know how to quantify this variable, but this flexibility is crucial to note and gauge in some manner for youth with behavioral disorders, because employer support is related to job success.

2. Psychometric assessment tools (IQ tests, personality tests) have only peripheral utility in the vocational assessment exercise and should not be used to make major decisions about the work skills of students with behavioral disorders. These instruments may be used as base measures and may provide some relevant data to augment the overall process. For example, IQ information and personality measures should be employed to gain a rough idea of a student's raw skills; but as stated previously, these results have weak relationships with success in job placements.

3. Structured interviews and observations of the students on the job can assist in identifying their requirements for work, their likes, and their dislikes. Of course, it must be noted that adolescents, particularly those who have minimal work experiences, are likely to change their work goals and desires many times as part of their development and exposure to different occupations. Thus, it is necessary to conduct this kind of evaluation periodically to document changes due to maturation and experience.

4. Most commercially available work sample systems do not possess sufficiently strong psychometric properties for use in school-based assessment programs. Of course, as the available work sites in a region become clear, it is possible to identify components of these systems that match these jobs and to develop locally based norms. For example, a particular work sample system may be a reasonable likeness of a production job in a particular town. To establish initial criterion levels of performance on this task, workers from these jobs can be administered the sample. As students are tested on the sample, it will also be possible to compare student performance to worker norms to gauge the potential of students to perform that kind of job. Similarly, after identifying available jobs in a community, it is also possible to construct and standardize work samples that reflect the composition of those specific jobs and their requirements. However, though work samples can be used as an introductory assessment tool, they must not be viewed as an end unto themselves. There are simply too many variables associated with the job setting that cannot be reproduced in an analog situation.

5. Multiple measures should be used in each of the four assessment phases, and it is also important to gather data from multiple informants (Achenbach, 1985; Campbell & Fiske, 1959; Kazdin, 1979) to examine situations from several different perspectives. Work supervisors, physicians, co-workers, family members, and other teachers may all supply important information for the student's vocational assessment.

6. The bulk of the vocational assessment for youth with behavioral disorders should be composed of situational assessments (Hursh & Kerns, 1988). In this technique, the client is placed in job situations and then his or her work skills and behavior are observed and measured (Kuhlman, 1975; McCray, 1982; Pruitt, 1976).

> The purpose of situational assessment is to systematically observe the individual's performance in relation to the characteristics of the work environment, and to systematically adjust work characteristics (tasks assigned, relations to others, amount and type of supervision, production demands) in order to identify the social and environmental factors that may promote or hinder work performance. . . . Situational assessment is not only a process of observing behavior, but is also a dynamic process of systematically altering work characteristics to observe work adjustment and performance. (Hursh & Kerns, 1988, p. 156)

Data from situational assessments may be gathered from rating scales of work behaviors completed on a frequent basis by work supervisors, rating scales of student's behaviors completed by co-workers or teachers, and behavioral observations of the student performing on the job. An example of segments of such a rating scale is provided in Figure 2 (Fredericks & Nishioka-Evans, 1987).

In summary, the vocational assessment of students with behavioral disorders should focus on the content and skills workers must exhibit in the workplace. Data should be gathered to both structure and evaluate the actual impact of the vocational education and community-based training program. Moreover, it is clear that special attention should be paid to the assessment of job-related social behavior, because these skills are critical to the vocational success of these students.

FIGURE 2
Situational Assessment Rating Form

ASSOCIATED WORK SKILLS CHECKLIST

Student: _____

Date: _____

Work-Related Behavior	Has Skill	Needs Training	Comments
1. Checks own work			
2. Corrects mistakes			
3. Works alone without disruptions for specified period with no contact from supervisor/teacher			
4. Works continuously at a job station for specified amount of time			
5. Safety:			
a. Uses appropriate safety gear			
b. Responds appropriately during fire drill			
c. follows safety procedures specific to classroom/shop			
d. Wears safe work clothing			
e. Cleans work area			
f. Identifies and avoids dangerous areas			
g. Responds appropriately to emergency situation (sickness, injury, etc.)			
6. Participates in work environment for specified periods of time			
7. Works in group situation without being distracted			
8. Works faster when asked to do so			
9. Completes work by specified time when told to do so			
10. Time Management:			
a. Comes to class/work for designated number of times per week			
b. Arrives at class/work on time			
c. Recognizes appropriate time to take break or lunch			
d. Recognizes appropriate time to change task			
e. Returns promptly from:			

Source: Adapted by permission from "Functional Curriculum," by H.D. Bud Fredericks, & V. Nishioka-Evans. In C. M. Nelson, R. Rutherford, & B. Wolford (Eds.), Special education in the criminal justice system (pp. 189–214). Columbus, OH: Merrill.

4. Social Skills Training for Obtaining a Job

Vocational training programs for youth with behavioral disorders should follow the sequence of skills needed in a natural setting, beginning with how to find a job and interviewing.

The Education for All Handicapped Children Act (P.L. 99-142) calls for the placement of students with disabilities in the least restrictive environment. In terms of the least restrictive environment, vocational placement may be the most challenging domain. That is, because of a person's behavioral disturbances, he or she might be an unlikely candidate for job hiring or retention. Unfortunately, there has been little research on this topic largely because a person with behavioral disorders is a difficult candidate for vocational placement, and some of the behaviors that he or she may exhibit are antisocial or dangerous. It is ironic that the very reason why such a person is in need of vocational training and experiences (i.e., deviant behaviors), is the very factor that mitigates against such placements. There are, however, a growing number of model projects and research efforts specific to the job-related social behavior of these persons.

Some social skills research has focused on the earlier stages of job procurement. The first stage of job procurement deals with finding a job. Hasazi et al. (1985) have found that youth with mild disabilities (including students with behavioral disorders) frequently found jobs through their family-friends network or on their own. Although job placement services have an effect, they do not result in obtaining nearly as many jobs as through leads from family and friends. Still, given the high unemployment rate of youth with mild disabilities, strategies are needed to connect people with jobs. Azrin and Besalel (1980) have developed the now well-known Job Club program. Job Club teaches the participant a variety of job procurement skills, taking the position that it is the job-seeker's responsibility to find his or her own employment. The behaviorally based procedure teaches the individual to identify particular jobs through newspapers and phone calls. Through continuous, protracted contacts, a list of jobs is assembled; and interviews are established. Though the approach has been used with great success with chronically unemployed, low functioning persons (Azrin & Philip, 1979), there has been little research to apply Job Club procedures directly to youth with BD. Adaptation and critical evaluation of the intervention are warranted for its impact on students with behavioral disorders and its "fit" within the school setting (e. g., Does the Job Club's structure need to be revised to mesh with class schedules?).

A second job procurement skill, job interviewing, also has been taught and researched with people with emotional disturbances. Job interviewing is a social skill that involves a didactic interaction between the personnel interviewer and the job seeker. Kelly has developed an individual (Furman, Geller, Simon, & Kelly, 1979) and a group (Kelly, J. A., Laughlin, Claiborne, & Patterson, 1979) training procedure for former psychiatric patients. The training procedure uses the typical behaviorally based components of social skill training (SST). That is, the trainer instructs and models the desired behaviors; the participants role play or rehearse the stipulated behaviors; and, finally, feedback (information or reward) is provided after the rehearsal. In both studies, three behaviors were targeted for training: providing information, expression of enthusiasm, and questions to the interviewer. Each of the behaviors was successively trained within a multiple baseline design. Before training, each of the behaviors appeared at a near zero rate. After the onset of training, the appearance of the targeted behaviors increased dramatically.

In SST, the importance of training behaviors during a role play is secondary to having these behaviors generalize to a real setting. In job interviewing, it would be critical to produce generalization from the role play to real job interviews. To approximate this situation, Kelly and his colleagues recruited actual personnel interviewers. Unstructured generalization probes simulated an actual job interview. Pre- and post-measures were taken of the participants' performance. In general, the participants' performance improved substantially from pretest to posttest. This change was noted in both the specific behaviors trained (e.g., enthusiasm) and in more global, social validity ratings (e.g., ambition, speech fluency, context appropriateness, and likelihood of being hired). The ultimate social validity criterion in job interviewing training is whether the participant obtains employment. In Kelly's group instruction study, five of the six participants obtained jobs. In Kelly's individual instruction study, two of the three participants became employed. Thus, Kelly and his colleagues have empirically demonstrated a relatively brief and effective training procedure for developing job interviewing social behaviors. This basic model appears to have applicability for youth with BD within school transition programs.

5. Social Skills Training for the Workplace

Training programs should teach social skills that will be needed in actual encounters on the job, including skills relating to interactions with work supervisors and co-workers and building relationships.

In addition to teaching job procurement skills, some work has been done in training social skills that will be needed in actual encounters on the job. Salzberg and his colleagues conducted a series of studies to demonstrate the acquisition and generalization of job-related social skills. In the first study, Warrenfeltz et al. (1981) taught four young people with behavioral disorders to make appropriate responses to instructions (e.g., "Put away those tools."). The students had to respond appropriately in a verbal and motoric fashion, and they were to avoid negative verbal responses like whining or refusing. A first "didactic" training condition taught the students to distinguish, define, and identify appropriate and inappropriate work-related social behaviors. Data were simultaneously collected in a simulated work setting in the school. Although the students learned each of the trained behaviors, they failed to generalize appropriate responses to instruction in the simulated setting. Next, a role-play and self-monitoring training condition was implemented. The students and teacher role-played vignettes that could occur in work settings. In addition, students self-monitored their social responses in the simulated setting. That is, students rated their social responses to the work supervisor. After successful acquisition, the role-play and self-monitoring conditions produced generalization of appropriate responses to instruction into the generalization setting. Impressively, response generalization was achieved for the untrained behavior of appropriate response to critical feedback, a skill critical for job tenure.

A subsequent study by the Salzberg group (Kelly, W. J., et al., 1983) similarly trained four young people with behavioral disorders to make appropriate responses to instruction. The investigation attempted to determine whether role playing or self-monitoring was causal in producing generalization. First, a role-play-only condition was introduced. Although the students acquired the social discrimination responses, they failed to display appropriate responses to instruction in the simulated, school generalization setting. Subsequently, a role-play plus self-monitoring condition induced both acquisition and generalization. These studies are unique and impressive in that they identified the critical training conditions to produce generalized social responding, but are limited in that they were not validated in competitive work settings.

Breen, Haring, Pitts-Conway, and Gaylord-Ross (1985) taught several social behaviors in an actual work setting. A group of four young people with serious emotional disturbance and autism had been working in a nursing home and a restaurant. The SST attempted to teach them a number of social behaviors in the break room of the workplace. Such behaviors included initiating a conversation, making small talk, and offering co-workers coffee or sugar. A training procedure used high school peers without disabilities to didactically role play the social exchange with the autistic youth. A script of the sequence of social behaviors in a typical exchange was task analyzed and rehearsed. Training took place in the same break setting, because the generalization was across persons (student peers to adult co-workers) and not settings. Breen et al. (1985) investigated the number of training peers required before generalization occurred with co-workers at breaktime. There were no consistent findings. One autistic student needed one peer trainer, two students required two peer trainers, and a fourth needed three peer trainers before generalization occurred with co-workers.

In a series of studies in England, Spence and her colleagues investigated SST procedures and the effects of the training on incarcerated adolescent boys. In an initial effort to identify key skill deficits, Spence (1981) conducted short (5-min) videotaped interviews with 70 subjects. Each of the boys was asked standard questions regarding school, life, hobbies, and career aspirations. Judges then rated each of the video interviews on 13 previously identified social skill variables (e.g., gestures, smiling, eye contact, amount spoken, interruptions, questions, initiations). The judges then rated each boy on four 10-point scales relating to their perceptions of the subject from the interviews: overall friendliness, anxiousness, general social skills, and employability. Measures of eye contact and verbal initiations were correlated to all four of the global ratings, particularly to employability. Other behaviors that were significantly correlated to employability ratings included amount spoken, questions asked, interruptions, and latency of response (this last skill area was negatively correlated to the rating). In sum, these results suggest that social skills for different content areas vary, but that these behavioral competencies can, and should, be identified to focus training and foster an effective intervention.

Two studies by Spence and Marziller examined both the short- and long-term effects of SST on male offenders. In the first study, on the immediate effects of SST on the social behavior of five adolescent males (Spence & Marziller, 1979), behavioral skill deficits were identified for each boy (e.g., seconds of eye contact, fiddling movements, head movements, questions). Interventions were then administered for each boy, using instructions, modeling, role playing, videotaped feedback, practice of the skills in the target setting, and social reinforcement. A multiple baseline design across behaviors was used to examine the effects of the intervention. Personal and third-party ratings, coupled with observational ratings of the specific behaviors on videotape interactions between the boys and the trainer, were used as the dependent measures. Overall, it was found that eye contact and verbal behaviors were amenable to change, but that listening behaviors were much harder to improve. Improvements in the altered behaviors were maintained at a 2-week, postintervention follow-up.

In the second and larger study, Spence and Marziller (1981) implemented an SST intervention with 76 adolescent, male offenders. Participants were assigned to one of three groups: SST, placebo control, or no-treatment control. The SST intervention consisted of 12 one-hour sessions. Behaviors that were taught were discrete social skills (e.g., eye contact) or more complex skills (e.g., dealing with bullying, interacting with police, making friends). Dependent measures included a staff questionnaire of each person's social functioning, a self-report questionnaire, and behavioral observation. A multiple baseline design across discrete behaviors was used to examine the effects of the intervention on these skills, and questionnaires were administered pre- and post-intervention to identify differences in social performance among the three groups. For the SST group, it was possible to effect positive change for most of the social skills that were trained. This behavioral improvement was maintained in a 3-month follow-up. Comparisons among the three groups at follow-up revealed that the SST group outperformed the other two groups on performance of the basic, discrete social skills. However, staff and social workers' questionnaires on each boy's friendliness, social behaviors, school and family relationships, anxiety and employability, and self-reports of criminal behavior and convictions demonstrated no differences among the groups. The authors concluded that SST in isolation may have limited value and that the procedure should be considered as part of a broader approach (a group home approach with multiple interventions).

Hazel, Schumaker, Sherman, and Sheldon-Wildgen (1981) developed a comprehensive curriculum package to train eight broad areas of social skills for antisocial, delinquent youth with learning disabilities. The program included instruction in giving positive feedback, giving negative feedback, accepting negative feedback, resisting peer pressure, negotiating conflict situations, following instructions, conversation, and personal problem solving. Through a behavioral analytic process (Goldfried & D'Zurilla, 1969), specific problems within these areas were identified; and discrete skill components, central to the successful social skill performance, were delineated (e.g., face the person, keep eye contact, ask if you can talk, tell the person how you feel). This content formed the basis of eight behavioral checklists that reflect skills critical in each of the eight domains. The curriculum used a structured learning approach in conjunction with videotapes demonstrating social problems and their resolution to train appropriate behaviors in these areas..

Three studies of the skill training procedure provide evidence that the intervention is effective for externalizing, court adjudicated male and female youths (Hazel et al., 1981, 1982; Schumaker, Hazel, Sherman, & Sheldon, 1982). In each, externalizing participants improved either on pre/posttest comparisons or on multiple baseline designs across behaviors. Moreover, behavioral changes were relatively durable, maintaining in one study for an 8-month time period (Hazel et al., 1982); and in one investigation evaluation of the training by participants and probation officers was positive.

Finally, other studies provide support for SST with youth with behavioral disorders in structured settings. For example, SST has been used to successfully modify aggressive behavior among adolescents in psychiatric hospitals (Elder, Edelstein, & Narick, 1979) and train appropriate social behavior among incarcerated adolescent boys in a custodial institution (Ollendick & Herson, 1979).

Investigations focusing on perceived social/cognitive deficits of externalizing, aggressive adolescents (Dodge, 1980; Platt et al., 1974; Slaby & Guerra, 1988; Spivack, Platt, & Shure, 1976), have studied the training of role-taking behaviors (Chandler, 1973); cognitive strategies (Foxx & Bittle, 1989; Sarason & Sarason, 1981); moral reasoning (Arbuthnot & Gordon, 1986; Niles, 1986); and a combination of behavioral, cognitive, and moral reasoning (Goldstein & Glick, 1987). Overall, studies using this social/cognitive approach (D'Zurilla, 1986; Meichenbaum, 1977; Spivack et al., 1976) were effective to some degree and are certainly reflective of an emerging trend among social skill instruction in special education (Harris, 1982) to foster skill acquisition and generalization of learned behaviors.

In summary, the research reviewed in this section indicated that SST techniques can be effective with youth with behavioral disorders. The bulk of this research has focused on externalizing students and has been geared toward general community adjustment skills, and not specifically to vocational or living settings. Although the results from the studies reviewed here are promising, it is apparent that this type of inquiry and intervention is in a very early stage of development. Much more work is necessary to examine and delineate powerful instructional techniques, develop training strategies that use the natural environment as a training component (e.g., the work setting), and to demonstrate the long-term effects of SST on social skills and overall adult adjustment. We should expect growth in this field because social skills are critical to successful job retention, indicate a satisfactory work life, and mediate to some degree social functioning in the community. It is our opinion that at least two areas need to be addressed to improve SST conducted with youth with behavioral disorders.

6. Necessary Directions for Social Skills Training

Social skills training should use a "process" approach and foster the formation of supportive relationships.

Process Approach

The first area needing extensive examination and research relates to the way in which social skills are trained. Past SST work has typically been behavioral component training. That is, antecedent modeling, response rehearsal, and consequent feedback have allied SST closely with the principles of applied behavior analysis. Trower (1984) has suggested that a "process" type of training should produce better generalization of social behaviors to target settings. Process SST emphasizes the use of cognitive activities. These cognitive processes include decoding the social context, delineating and deciding on behavior choices, and self-monitoring and self-evaluating one's performance. To illustrate what a cognitive-behavioral training package *may* look like, a hypothetical example follows.

When training students with behavioral disorders to request assistance from a vocational supervisor, the trainer would begin with a discussion of the importance of such behavior and a call for participants to volunteer instances when they have asked supervisors for help or when they have had problems making such requests. "Real life" problems volunteered by the participants would be used to focus training. The trainees would be introduced to the cognitive behavioral approach, and one of the social problems would serve as a practice situation where the interaction is role-played. Depending on the sophistication and level of training of the group, the role-play may be conducted by the trainers only, a trainer and one trainee, or trainees only. The trainees would be required to critique the interaction and to outline the specifics of the situation to be dealt with in the interaction. Once the problem is delineated, possible behavioral solutions, or alternatives, to the interaction would be generated and discussed by the group. A "correct" answer or group of correct answers would be identified by the trainees based on the discussion. The trainer would then try to foster an understanding of the effectiveness of the responses for the particular situation among the participants.

These behaviors would then be practiced in the lesson through a variety of role-play and behavioral principles, including video recording and critique of each trainee's behavior in the practice situations. To facilitate generalization of the learned behavior to the work setting, trainees would be required to practice with more than one confederate; in all instances, attention would be focused on the work environment in which a trainee is placed currently. Also, at the end of the lesson, each of the trainees would be assigned "homework," that is, a specific social skill to practice away from the lesson in the work setting with the appropriate "other" (e. g., a work supervisor or co-workers).

In line with this approach, Larson (1984) has developed a social thinking curriculum for young people with behavioral disorders. A group of students at a residential facility was taught to formulate problems, generate alternatives, select solutions, implement behaviors, and self-evaluate their performance. Larson and Gerber (1987) reported that the youth successfully learned these cognitive-behavioral skills. Furthermore, the youth substantially reduced their frequency of problem behaviors in other parts of their lives. Problem-solving programs like Larson's hold promise for social skills training in vocational and community contexts.

Fostering Relationships

A second subject that demands attention is relationship development. Relationship development may have some common goals with SST, but it proceeds in a different manner. Rather than focusing on discrete behaviors, relationship development examines the roles people play at work and tries to develop more intensive relationships. It is hoped that a certain number of acquaintances and friendships will develop naturally during the person's job tenure. Still, because some jobs are performed in relative isolation, or the behaviors or the stigmatizing label of a person with behavioral disturbance may lead co-workers to avoid contact with him or her, it may be necessary to carry out interventions that foster the formation of relationships.

If there is a job coach present at the work site, one of the coach's roles may be to analyze the social network of the workplace. The job coach or counselor could then design ways to integrate the student into this social network. For example, some co-workers may be interested in befriending and supporting the student. Such support and friendships may develop naturally. In other cases, co-workers might need to be encouraged or prompted to form relationships. In some situations, a co-worker may be formally designated as a benefactor for the student. For example, the Pathways Program for workers with developmental disabilities in England (Porterfield & Gathercole, 1985) formally designates a co-worker to be a mentor or benefactor. The benefactor may then orient, instruct, integrate, and support the worker with disabilities.

One tangible way to integrate the worker is to analyze the social rituals at the workplace. Often a group of workers have monthly birthday parties for one of their members. It would be important that the youth with behavioral disorders participate in such rituals to become integrated into workplace subgroups. A benefactor, job coach, or counselor may facilitate such social integration.

Integration into the social network at the workplace is important for several reasons. Becoming a productive worker usually entails working cooperatively with one's co-workers. Also, the quality of one's work experience (whether the individual "likes" the work) is likely to be related to the formation of friendships in the employment setting. Finally, some research has shown social networks to offer social support, which provides a buffer against stress (Cohen, S., & Willis, 1985). The stress-buffer notion should have important implications for youth with BD. Competitive jobs place many pressures on employees to work rapidly, perform complex tasks, and adapt to changing tasks and demands. Such pressures may induce stress on the student and may threaten his or her mental health, cause the worker to resign, or diminish the quality of his or her work experience. We are just beginning to understand the social ecology of the workplace. The development of relationship information and SST interventions should enhance the vocational potential of people with behavioral disorders. Furthermore, the complementary intervention focus on the individual and the surrounding ecology is consistent with a comprehensive ecological perspective.

Gaylord-Ross, Park, Cameto, and Tappe (1990) have advanced an ecosocial perspective to explain the interplay between individual and ecological social variables. The ecosocial notion is congruent with the ecosystematic view developed by Hobbs (1982) for youth with behavioral disorders. Figure 3 presents the four levels of social reality in the ecosocial model.

For each level, there are corresponding interrelationships that have been validated in past research and practice. The macro level represents large-scale setting variables that may influence social integration. Vocationally, an agency, region, or state might implement a systems change effort to convert from a sheltered workshop system to a community-based one. With such changes, youth in transition would have a dramatically different quality of work life between a workshop and competitive work environment. The next, relationship level of social reality articulates the different networks in a person's life. For example, an individual has two acquaintances and one friend at work. The same person may have many, few, or no relations with persons in the other domains of school, residence, or community. These persons may have different types of relationships and offer varying kinds of support, for example, instructional and emotional.

Relationship interventions in the workplace are just beginning to be explored. Park et al., (1990) have had co-worker benefactors participate in a 6-week relationship intervention. The co-workers generate activities that could better socially integrate the employee with disabilities at the workplace. The third, social interaction level of social

FIGURE 3
Ecosocial Model

THE ECOSOCIAL SYSTEM

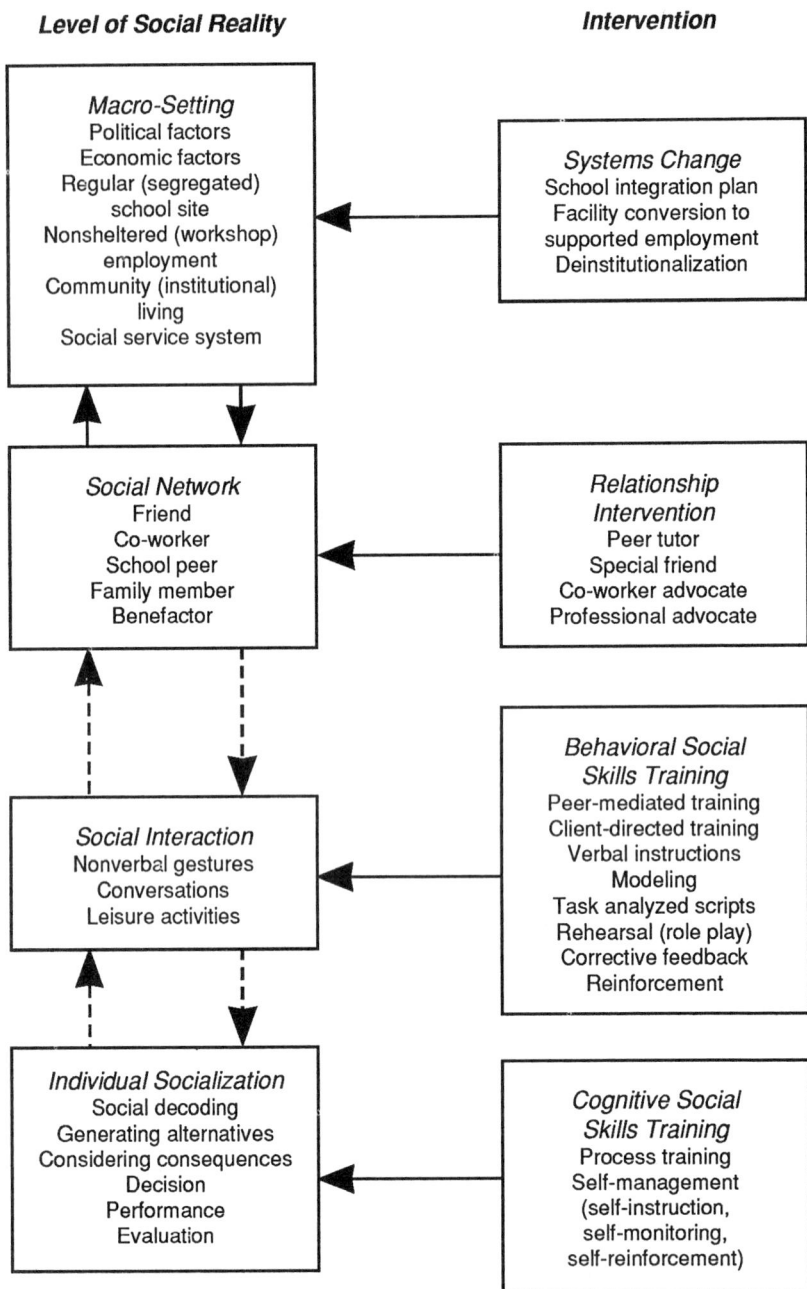

Level of Social Reality   *Intervention*

Macro-Setting
Political factors
Economic factors
Regular (segregated)
school site
Nonsheltered (workshop)
employment
Community (institutional)
living
Social service system

Systems Change
School integration plan
Facility conversion to
supported employment
Deinstitutionalization

Social Network
Friend
Co-worker
School peer
Family member
Benefactor

*Relationship
Intervention*
Peer tutor
Special friend
Co-worker advocate
Professional advocate

Social Interaction
Nonverbal gestures
Conversations
Leisure activities

*Behavioral Social
Skills Training*
Peer-mediated training
Client-directed training
Verbal instructions
Modeling
Task analyzed scripts
Rehearsal (role play)
Corrective feedback
Reinforcement

Individual Socialization
Social decoding
Generating alternatives
Considering consequences
Decision
Performance
Evaluation

*Cognitive Social
Skills Training*
Process training
Self-management
(self-instruction,
self-monitoring,
self-reinforcement)

reality is the one most frequently investigated and previously described in this chapter. The intraindividual, cognitive level of social reality focuses on social problem-solving processes and interventions (cf. Park & Gaylord-Ross, 1989). A comprehensive vocational-socialization program should address all levels of social reality. Fortunately, an increasing number of research and demonstration efforts are documenting a wide range of efficacious ecosocial programs.

7. Model Program I. The Sprague Program

This model uses a resource room/mainstreaming approach with a curriculum emphasis on independent living, social interaction, and vocational skills that are actually taught in in vivo settings where they will be used.

For almost 10 years, teaching research (TR) staff have been working with secondary students with behavioral disorders in a high school program located at Sprague High School in Salem, Oregon (Nishioka-Evans, 1987). The students referred to this program are among the most difficult served by the Children Services Division of the state of Oregon. In addition to behavioral disorders, most students present with other mild cognitive disabilities (e.g., mild mental retardation). Further, most of these students exhibit extreme deviant behaviors (e.g., stealing, prostitution, physical aggression) that have made it impossible for them to be maintained in their homes and/or community schools, hence their referral to this site. Long-term follow-up of the 48 students who have participated in the program indicates that 65% are in successful school or work placements 1 year after leaving the program. This is a notable result, especially in light of the serious problems they exhibited before entering Sprague.

Between 10 and 14 male and female students are involved in the program at any one time, with the average stay being 1 to 2 years. There are two main residences for the participants, a group home and a supervised apartment living complex operated by TR, while some students live in a foster care residence or, in very rare cases, with their natural parents.

The school component takes the form of a resource room in a regular school facility, with students being mainstreamed into other classes as appropriate; but the core of the school program is based on a functional curriculum (Fredericks & Nishioka-Evans, 1987). This instructional model is *not* focused toward traditional, academic classes. Rather, it emphasizes practical learning grounded in the requirements of working and living in the community and uses a task analytic, behavioral teaching approach. Broadly, instruction is provided in three major content areas: independent living, social interaction, and vocational skills. Delineation of skills taught in the three domains is provided in Figure 4 (Fredericks & Nishioka-Evans, 1987). Particular attention is given in preparing students for the living and work settings they will move to upon leaving the program, and to involve all appropriate service agencies and resources in the eventual movement of the student to another setting.

What makes this program unique, and quite possibly the reasons for its effectiveness, relates to its emphasis on teaching these functional skills in the community. This means that independent living skills are taught and learned in actual residences, that vocational skills are practiced in community-based work settings, and that correct social behaviors for community integration are learned and rehearsed in the work, living, and social environments in which they naturally occur. Of course, initial instruction takes place in the classroom, but to be truly effective, the primary intervention is grounded in the actual demands of living and working in the community.

> Certain skills can be practiced or role played in the classroom but they must eventually be generalized in the community in "real" situations. For instance, one can practice a job interview in a classroom but one must actually demonstrate those skills in a *bona fide* job interview. Certainly the use of the calculator can best be taught in a classroom, but the use of a calculator to figure out the costs of items in stores, totaling the balance in a checkbook, or budgeting one's money must be eventually demonstrated in the "real" world. *There are no functional living skills, social skills, or vocational skills that can be learned solely in a classroom environment.* Each must be practiced in the actual community or situation in which the skill is to be used. (Fredericks & Nishioka-Evans, 1987, pp. 195–196)

In line with this community-based instructional philosophy, a five-phase system of vocational instruction is employed. Each higher phase is more demanding than the previous one, as movement through the system progresses from closely supervised training in unpaid vocational sites to unsupervised and paid work in competitive jobs in the community. These phases and their respective requirements are presented in Figure 5.

Untrained, inexperienced students are likely to begin their vocational training at Level I. Students who demonstrate exceptional work skills and appropriate job-related behaviors may advance through the hierarchy to as high as Level V. Of course, advancement is sporadic with such training, and most students do not progress cleanly and without

FIGURE 4
Structure of the Functional Curricula for the Sprague Program

The scope of *independent living skills* includes the following:

Telephone skills
Newspaper skills
Transportation skills
    Public transportation utilization
    Car ownership and management
Money skills
    Budgeting
    Bill paying
    Banking
    Shopping skills
    Food
    Clothes
    Other
    Menu planning
    Cooking skills
    Home and yard maintenance
    Survival reading (Being able to read signs in supermarkets,
        newspapers, clothes labels and size, job applications,
        recipes, schedules, etc.)
    Use of the calculator
    Measurement skills
    Leisure time skills

The *social skills* domain includes:

Human Awareness
    Self-esteem
    Personal rights
    Relationships
    Feelings
    Solving problems
    Sexual knowledge
Communication
    Compliments
    Conversation
    Assertiveness
    Listening skills
    Speaking skills

The *vocational* domain of the functional curriculum includes:

Applying for a job
Learning how to interview for a job
Performance on the job
Using correct social skills on the job

Source: Adapted by permission from "Functional Curriculum," by H.D. Bud Fredericks, & V. Nishioka-Evans. In C. M. Nelson, R. Rutherford, & B. Wolford (Eds.), *Special education in the criminal justice system* (pp. 189–214). Columbus, OH: Merrill.

FIGURE 5
Phase System of Job Placement

PHASE I "The Learning Phase"

1. Is supervised and trained on all tasks and duties by vocational trainer.
2. Learns various job duties required by job site.
3. Learns and follows all rules and regulations as posted by vocational site.
4. Begins to identify and work on skills and behaviors exhibitied at work site.
5. All data from skill and behavior program to be collected and recorded by trainer.
6. Begins to explore transportation options such as city buses, bicycling, walking.
7. May begin bus training if appropriate and available.
8. Maintains a minimum of 3 working hours per week.
9. All consequences and contacts to be handled by trainer.

PHASE II "The Responsibility Phase"

1. Trainer to make intermittent quality checks while remaining on job site.
2. Begins to maintain various job duties independently.
3. Begins to follow all rules and regulations of job site independently.
4. Begins to set own goals with trainer and watches own behavior.
5. All data from skill and behavior program to be collected and recorded by trainer.
6. Begins transporting self using public transporation if available with trainer guidance and supervision.
7. Uses vocational time wisely; maintains satisfactory work rate and quality.
8. Will maintain at least 5 working hours per week.
9. Begins to receive and respond to occasional feedback from employer.
10. All consequences and majority of contact to be handled by trainer.

PHASE III "The Transition Phase"

1. Trainer not at job site, makes intermittent quality checks.
2. Independent in all job duties and tasks.
3. Follows all rules and regulations of job site independently.
4. Works toward vocational goals and maintains own behaviors.
5. Skill and behavior data monitored with forms completed by employer and trainer.
6. Independent transportation to and from work.
7. Maintains work quality equal to that of regular employee.
8. Will maintain at least 10 working hours per week.
9. Responds to employer in all job related matters.
10. Consequences given by either trainer or employer, with the emphasis on employer.

PHASE IV "The Independent Phase"

1. Trainer to make intermittent quality checks by phone.
2. Independent in all job duties and tasks.
3. Independently follows all rules and regulations of job site.
4. Continues to work toward vocational goals and monitors own behaviors.
5. No formal behavior programs.
6. Independent to and from work site.
7. Maintains work quality equal to that of regular employee.
8. Will maintain 10–15 working hours per week.
9. Responds to employer in all job related matters.
10. Consequences given by employer.
11. Eligible for placement in paid employment with trainer support.

PHASE V "The Employability Phase"

1. Trainer assists with administrative issues.
2. Employer trains and manages.
3. Reaches vocational goals.
4. Independent transportation to and from work.
5. Maintains 20 working hours per week for 1 year.
6. Independently secures paid employment.

incident through the five employment phases. In fact, failure is common, as evidenced by the work histories of 15 students presented in Table 1. Clearly, a critical element of success for participants in this program, and probably for other youth with behavioral disorders as well, is persistence in continuing to place students in vocational positions.

In the fall of 1989, TR began a supported work model demonstration project, similar to the Sprague model, at the Children's Farm Home in Corvallis, Oregon (Fredericks & Bullis, 1989), a program that serves adolescents who have either been adjudicated or who are wards of the court system. Almost all these youth have an unsuccessful school history, behavioral disorders, and many have learning disabilities. This effort is funded through federal dollars designated for the supported work initiative. Thus, participants in the program strive to work 20 hours per week in a paid, competitive job. Accordingly, the major focus of the project is on students who are ready to enter Level IV or V of the employability levels. Most students are older (16 to 18 years of age), with a degree of work experience, and with at least some of the appropriate skills necessary to work competitively. This project is one of the first to deal specifically with this group under the umbrella of the supported work initiative.

8. Model Program II. The Career Ladder Program

This program uses a community classroom model to conduct work experience training in a variety of training sites during the 10th, 11th, and 12th grades.

The Career Ladder Program (CLP) is a longitudinal transition program serving youth with mild disabilities in San Francisco. Whereas the majority of the students in the program are classified as learning disabled, approximately 10% of the youth are classified as behaviorally disordered. Also, many of the youth with learning disabilities have accompanying behavioral problems. Therefore, we believe that the program components of CLP would be applicable to students with BD.

The CLP (Siegel, Gaylord-Ross, Greener, & Robert, 1990) ideally starts with a semester work experience during the 10th grade. Some students begin in 11th and some in 12th grade. The 10th grader spends 3 half school days at a particular work site. The CLP has identified a variety of work training sites, including hospitals, office buildings, warehouses, restaurants, and so forth. The 12th grade students spend 4 half-days at the work site. It is designed so that students will rotate

TABLE 1

TABLE 1
Brief History of Vocational Placements for Students

Student	Placement	Length of Placement	Reasons for Termination
1	N. S. Khalsa	3 mos.	Placement Complete
	Salem Public Library	4 mos.	Fired: Theft—Training Decision
	Capitol Motor Inn (Maid)	1 1/2 mos.	Placement Complete
	Capitol Motor Inn	2 mos.	Fired: Unsafe Behavior (Kitchen) Employer Request
	Salem Garden Supply	1 mo.	Fired: Attendance Problems Due to Runaway Behavior—Training Decision
	Southside Veterinary	2 mos.	Placement Complete
	N. S. Khalsa	7 mos.	Fired: Unsafe Behavior— Training Decision
2	Roth's IGA	3 mos.	Placement Complete
	Tamale Factory	3 days	Student Request
	Pet Peddler	2 mos.	Placement Complete
	Pietro's	5 mos.	Fired: Theft—Employer Request
	Speedy Mart	2 mos.	Ongoing
3	Executive Motor Inn	1 mo.	Placement Complete
	Kidspace	7 mos.	Student Moved
	N. S. Khalsa	3 days	Student Moved
4	N. S. Khalsa	1 mo.	Fired: Aggression— Employer Request
	Jory Hill Stables	1 mo.	Placement Ended
	Roth's IGA	7 mos.	Ongoing
5	Round Table Pizza	2 mos.	Ongoing
6	Southside Veterinary	14 mos.	Placement Complete
	Pietro's	2 mos.	Placement Complete
7	Roth's IGA	6 mos.	Placement Complete
	Associated Animal Hospital	3 1/2 mos.	Fired: Attendance— Training Decision
	Southside Veterinary	1/2 mo.	Student Request
	N. S. Khalsa	2 mos.	Placement Complete
	Tamale Factory	3 1/2 mos.	Store Closed

(continued)

TABLE 1 (continued)

Student	Placement	Length of Placement	Reasons for Termination
8	Student Services	4 mos.	Placement Complete
	Oregon School for the Blind	2 1/2 mos.	Placement Complete
	Mirage	2 mos.	Ongoing
9	Hospice	6 mos.	Ongoing
	N. S. Khalsa	7 days	Ongoing
10	Saga Foods	10 mos.	Fired: Theft— Employer Request
11	Sunnyside Care Center	6 mos.	Placement Complete
12	Tamale Factory	1 1/2 mos.	Fired: Poor Hygiene— Training Decision
	Smith Auditorium	8 mos.	Placement Complete
	Transformed Plastics	2 wks.	Hired Relief (Ongoing)
13	Volunteer Services	3 mos.	Placement Complete
	Salem Public Library		Placement Complete
	A Cut Above	2 mos.	Placement Complete
	Sunnyside Care Center	2 mos.	Placement Complete
	Sunnyside Pizza	5 mos.	Store Closed
14	Motor Pool	5 1/2 mos.	Placement Complete
	Albertson's	8 mos.	Fired: Co-worker Problems—Employer Request
	Judson's Plumbing	1 mo.	Placement Complete
15	Sunshine Pizza	4 mos.	Placement Complete
	Heliotrope	2 wks.	Fired: Unsafe Behavior— Employer Request
	Albertson's	4 mos.	Fired: Theft—Training Decision
	N. S. Khalsa	4 mos.	Student Moved

through different work settings through their secondary years (Gaylord-Ross, Forte, Storey, Gaylord-Ross, & Jameson, 1987). This schedule permits a formative assessment of the pupil's vocational abilities and preferences across different work ecologies.

The CLP uses a community classroom model (Gaylord-Ross, Forte, & Gaylord-Ross, 1986) to conduct work experience training, with four to six students attending a work site. One instructor (a teacher or para-professional) supervises the small group of students. Initially, the students are taught job tasks at a single site in the business. Over the semester, the students are dispersed throughout the work site. The instructor moves around the site, supervising each student. The instructor also attempts to turn over supervision to co-workers in that setting. The instructor facilitates social interactions and friendly development between students and co-workers. Data are carefully collected on the student' job performance by the instructors, co-workers, and the students themselves.

In addition to their community work experience, the students spend an additional half-day at a career laboratory. A 15-week career education curriculum is implemented (Siegel et al., 1990). The lab addresses such topics as career opportunities, general work behaviors, social skills, job procurement, and job retention. Students also discuss their experience at the work site. A problem-solving approach (D'Zurilla, 1986) to work issues is used in discussing and developing strategies for work and life issues.

The CLP has a unique postsecondary program component. Students exiting from school are referred to transition specialists who provide an array of vocational services. Their immediate charge is to place the trainee into permanent employment. Many students obtain permanent employment at the work site where they were trained as seniors, and others are placed in other jobs. The transition specialist provides ongoing follow-up to graduates with services such as informal counseling, referral to continuing education, social skills training, on-the-job crisis intervention, family support, and referral to intensive counseling. The CLP has served up to 200 students with impressive outcomes. The structure and supportive nature of the program (as well as the inclusion of students with varying degrees of behavioral disorders) supports its application with the target population of this monograph.

9. Key Elements of Transition Programs

A successful transition program infuses vocational preparation activities into the academic curriculum, provides networks with support agencies and services, and provides realistic training experiences in competitive work settings. Involving the business community in the job training program may be the key element in successful transition.

Several factors are common to both model programs described in the previous sections. First, both programs emphasize employment and inundate the academic setting with vocational preparation activities and opportunities. Vocational instruction is not viewed as an "add on," but as the primary focus of the programs, in combination with pragmatic academic instruction. Second, networking among support agencies and services is an integral part of each program, and a clear transition process is articulated. Finally, both programs include extensive use of actual vocational placements in competitive work settings to offer realistic training experiences and to promote the transfer of skills learned in the academic setting or another work setting to novel, realistic environments. Such an approach mandates that the community and competitive employment settings become the learning environments for these students. This emphasis, that is, training youth with behavioral disorders in community settings, is unique in contemporary practice.

Employment success has often been viewed as the primary determinant of successful transition (Will, 1984). The typical focus has been on improving educational and service programs to enhance transition. Yet, the business community, rather than service programs, may hold the real key to successful employment. After all, it is the employer who hires, retains, promotes, and fires. It may be useful then to examine some of the business variables that affect youth in transition.

A pressing business need in the country is for a qualified workforce. The productivity growth rate in the United States has dropped precipitously in the past two decades, from 2% to 0.5%. In many ways, this decline reflects the inefficiency of American workers. Effective vocational training and placement programs can guarantee the employer that a productive and efficient worker will be obtained. The supported employment initiative and resulting service programs have used on-the-job instructors to ensure that work tasks are successfully completed. Such quality control of worker output is particularly appealing to employers. In fact, Halpern (1973) reported that the participation of efficacious high school vocational programs is a powerful variable influencing successful employment, even in settings and locales experiencing high rates of unemployment.

Embedded within the productivity issues is the matter of literacy in the workplace. Businesses often report that their employees are semi-illiterate or illiterate. This has led some employers to have work completed overseas. More progressively, many employers have instituted basic academic skill training to upgrade the quality of their workforce. Unfortunately, only 17% of young people with behavioral disorders are participating in postsecondary education (Neel et al., 1988). This lack of participation greatly limits the potential for improving academic and other skills. Vocational education programs at the school and postschool levels must incorporate literacy and basic mathematics skills in their curriculum.

Besides focusing on getting jobs, young people with disabilities must access positions with upward mobility. In fact, in the CLP many participants stated that they would not accept low-paying jobs that were headed nowhere. Thus, the CLP entered training agreements with large corporations whereby graduates might assume substantive positions in those companies. Substantive positions are characterized by full-time employment; benefits packages; and, most important, upward mobility. The term *career ladder* denotes that the trainees enter career paths with increasing pay, status, and skill levels. With this career ladder package in place, many students opted for and completed the entire CLP process.

A new development in the field may reverse this basic placement arrangement. *Corporate initiative* programs have a company start and promote the training of persons with disabilities. Thus, the business approaches an educational agency and explains its program for job and training opportunities. With jobs promised, it is likely that the service program will respond. In a best-case scenario, the company will also take the lead in on-the-job training and its funding. Corporate initiatives hold a promise for aggressive, effective, and cost beneficial employment programs for youth with behavioral disorders.

Summary

This monograph highlights important activities and program components that should be present in effective services for youth with behavioral disorders. A comprehensive vocational assessment should identify pupil preferences, abilities, motivational characteristics, and instructional designs. A longitudinal vocational program should be designed to include a postschool, vocational safety net of services. The vocational education should include a series of community-based work experiences in which general work skills are mastered. It should also mainstream the student with disabilities into appropriate occupational training courses. Furthermore, necessary academic skills must be infused into vocational activities. A career education curriculum should focus on job-search and job-keeping skills, and particular attention should be given to social skills relevant to the workplace. Of great import, the vocational programs must be coordinated with, if not initiated by, the business community. Such protracted business-education relationships tend to engender substantive jobs for career ladders. The business takes ownership of the vocational enterprise and is likely to make the transitional accommodations necessary to employ youth with behavioral disorders.

There is no question that these approaches will improve the vocational skills, and ultimate success, of youth with behavioral disorders. However, this is a difficult group with whom to work; and our knowledge base in this field is, at this point, sketchy. We are hopeful that more empirical and model demonstration projects will be initiated in this area to expand this foundation. Only through such efforts will we be able to assist these students to realize their full potential within our society.

References

Achenbach, T. (1966). The classification of children's psychiatric syndromes: A factor analytic study. *Psychological Monographs, 80,* 1–37.

Achenbach, T. (1985). *Assessment and taxonomy of child and adolescent psychopathology.* Beverly Hills, CA: Sage.

Achenbach, T., & McConaughy, S. (1987). *Empirically based assessment of child and adolescent psychopathology.* Beverly Hills, CA: Sage.

Anthony, W. (1979). *Principles of psychiatric rehabilitation.* Baltimore: University Park Press.

Arbuthnot, J., & Gordon, D. (1986). Behavioral and cognitive effects of a moral reasoning development intervention for high-risk behavior disordered adolescents. *Journal of Consulting and Clinical Psychology, 54,* 208–216.

August, G., Stewart, M., & Holmes, C. (1983). A four-year follow-up of hyperactive boys with and without conduct disorder. *British Journal of Psychiatry, 143,* 192–198.

Azrin, N. H., & Besalel, V. A. (1980). *Job club counselor's manual: A behavioral approach to vocational counseling.* Baltimore: University Park Press.

Azrin, N., & Philip, R. (1979). The job club method for the job handicapped: A comparative outcome study. *Rehabilitation Counseling Bulletin, 23,* 144–145.

Billert, E., & White, W. (1989). Comparing special education and vocational rehabilitation in serving persons with specific learning disabilities. *Rehabilitation Counseling Bulletin, 33,* 4–17.

Bishop, J. (1989). *Vocational education for at-risk youth: How can it be made more effective?* Ithaca, NY: Cornell University.

Braaten, S., Rutherford, R., & Evans, W. (Eds.). (1985). *Programming for adolescents with behavioral disorders.* (Vol. 2). Reston, VA: Council for Exceptional Children.

Braaten, S., Rutherford, R., & Kardash, C. (Eds.). (1985a). *Programming for adolescents with behavioral disorders.* (Vol. 1). Reston, VA: Council for Exceptional Children.

Breen, C., Haring, T., Pitts-Conway, V., & Gaylord-Ross, R. (1985). The training and generalization of social interaction at two job sites in the natural environment. *Journal of the Association for Persons with Severe Handicaps, 10,* 41–50.

Bullis, M., Bull, B., & Johnson, P. (1990). *Review of empirical research on the school-to-community transition of behaviorally disordered adolescents.* Manuscript submitted for publication, Teaching Research, Monmouth, OR.

Bullis, M., & Foss, G. (1986). Assessing the employment-related interpersonal competence of mildly mentally retarded workers. *American Journal of Mental Deficiency, 91,* 433–450.

Bullis, M., & Fredericks, H. D. B. (1988). *Development, standardization, and validation of a measure of job-related social behavior for SED adolescents.* Funded grant proposal, Field Initiated Research Studies, Office of Special Education Programs.

Bullis, M., Nishioka-Evans, V., & Fredericks, H. D. B. (1990). *Overview of the development of two measures of job-related social behavior for behaviorally disordered adolescents.* Unpublished manuscript, Teaching Research, Monmouth, OR.

Butler-Nalin, P., & Padilla, C. (1989). *Dropouts: The relationship of student characteristics, behaviors, and performance for special education students.* Menlo Park, CA: SRI International.

Campbell, D., & Fiske, D. (1959). Convergent and discriminant validation by the multitrait-multimethod matrix. *Psychological Bulletin, 54,* 81–105.

Chadsey-Rusch, J. (1986). Identifying and teaching valued social behaviors. In F. Rusch (Ed.), *Competitive employment: Issues and strategies* (pp. 273–289). Baltimore: Paul H. Brookes.

Chandler, M. (1973). Egocentrism and antisocial behavior: The assessment and training of social perspective training skills. *Developmental Psychology, 9,* 326–332.

Cobb, B. (1983). A curriculum-based approach to vocational assessment. *Teaching Exceptional Children, 15*(9), 216–219.

Cobb, B., & Lakin, D. (1985). Assessment and placement of handicapped pupils into secondary vocational education programs. *Focus on Exceptional Children, 17*(7), 1–14.

Cohen, B., & Anthony, W. (1984). Functional assessment in psychiatric rehabilitation. In A. Halpern & M. Fuhrer (Eds.), *Functional assessment in rehabilitation* (pp. 79–100). Baltimore: Paul H. Brookes.

Cohen, S., & Willis, T. A. (1985). Stress, social support, and the buffering hypothesis. *Psychological Bulletin, 98*(2), 310–357.

Cook, J., Solomon, M., & Mock, L. O. (1988). *What happens after the first job placement: Vocational transitioning among severely emotionally disturbed and behavior disordered adolescents.* Chicago, IL: Thresholds Research Institute.

Cowen, E., Pederson, A., Babijian, H., Izzo, L., & Troust, M. (1973). Long-term follow-up of early detected vulnerable children. *Journal of Consulting and Clinical Psychology, 41*, 438–446.

Davis, G., & Leitenberg, H. (1987). Adolescent sex offenders. *Psychological Bulletin, 101*, 417–427.

Dellario, D., Goldfield, E., Farkas, M., & Cohen, M. (1984). Functional assessment of psychiatrically disabled adults. In A. Halpern & M. Fuhrer (Eds.), *Functional assessment in rehabilitation* (pp. 239–252). Baltimore: Paul H. Brookes.

DeStefano, L. (1987). The use of standardized assessment in supported employment. In L. DeStefano & F. Rusch (Eds.), *Supported employment in Illinois: Assessment methodology and research issues* (pp. 55–98). Champaign, IL: Transition Institute.

Dishion, T., Loeber, R., Stouthamer-Loeber, M., & Patterson, G. (1984). Skills deficits and male adolescent delinquency. *Journal of Abnormal Child Psychology, 12*, 37–54.

Dodge, K. (1980). Social cognition and children's aggressive behavior. *Child Development, 51*, 162–170.

D'Zurilla, T. (1986). *Problem solving therapy.* New York: Springer.

Edgar, E. (1987). Secondary programs in special education: Are many of them justifiable? *Exceptional Children, 53*, 555–561.

Edgar, E. (1988). Employment as an outcome for mildly handicapped students: Current status and future directions. *Focus on Exceptional Children, 21*(1), 1–8.

Edgar, E., & Levine, P. (1987). *Special education students in transition 1976-1986.* Unpublished manuscript, Seattle, WA: University of Washington.

Elder, J., Edelstein, B., & Narick, M. (1979). Adolescent psychiatric patients: Modifying aggressive behavior with social skills training. *Behavior Modification, 3*, 161–178.

Farrington, D. (1986). The sociocultural context of childhood disorders. In H. Quay and J. Werry (Eds.), *Psychopathological disorders of childhood* (3rd ed.) (pp. 391–422). New York: Wiley.

Fink, A., & Kokasa, C. (1983). *Career education for behavior disordered students*. Reston, VA: Council for Exceptional Children.

Foss, G., Walker, H., Todis, B., Lyman, G., & Smith, C. (1986). *A social competence model for community employment settings*. Eugene, OR: University of Oregon.

Foxx, R., & Bittle, R. (1989). *Thinking it through. Teaching a problem-solving strategy for community living*. Champaign, IL: Research Press.

Fredericks, H. D. B., & Bullis, M. (1989). *A community-based, supported work program for SED adolescents*. Funded grant proposal, Rehabilitation Services Administration.

Fredericks, H. D. B., & Nishioka-Evans, V. (1987). Functional Curriculum. In C. M. Nelson, R. B. Rutherford, & B. I. Wolford (Eds.), *Special education in the criminal justice system* (pp. 189–214). Columbus, OH: Merrill.

Freedman, B., Donahoe, C., Rosenthal, L., Schlundt, D., & McFall, R. (1978). A social-behavioral analysis of skill deficits in delinquent and nondelinquent boys. *Journal of Consulting and Clinical Psychology, 46*, 1448–1462.

Frey, W. (1984). Functional assessment in the '80s. In A. Halpern & M. Fuhrer (Eds.), *Functional assessment in rehabilitation* (pp. 11–44). Baltimore: Paul H. Brookes.

Furman, W., Geller, M. I., Simon, S. J., & Kelly, J. A. (1979). Teaching job interviewing skills to adolescent patients through a behavior rehearsal procedure. *Behavior Therapy, 10*, 157–167.

Gaffney, L. R., & McFall, R. (1981). A comparison of social skills in delinquent and nondelinquent adolescent girls using a behavioral role-playing inventory. *Journal of Consulting and Clinical Psychology, 49*, 959–967.

Gaylord-Ross, R. (1986). *Vocational placement of mildly handicapped adolescents*. Funded proposal, OSERS.

Gaylord-Ross, R. (Ed.). (1988). *Vocational education for persons with handicaps*. Mountain View, CA: Mayfield.

Gaylord-Ross, C., Forte, J., & Gaylord-Ross, R. (1986). The community classroom: Technological vocational training for students with serious handicaps. *Career Development for Exceptional Individuals, 9*, 24–33.

Gaylord-Ross, R., Forte, J., Storey, K., Gaylord-Ross, C., & Jameson, D. (1987). Community-referenced instruction in technological work settings. *Exceptional Children, 54*, 112–120.

Gaylord-Ross, R., Park, H., Cameto, R., & Tappe, P. (1990). Ecosocial development: Considerations of social skills, social support, and quality of life. In R. Gaylord-Ross et al. (Eds.), *Readings in ecosocial development*. San Francisco: San Francisco State University.

Gaylord-Ross, R., Siegel, S., & Bullis, M. (1990). *Vocational education of emotionally disturbed youth*. Manuscript submitted for publication.

Goldfried, M., & D'Zurilla, T. (1969). A behavioral-analytic model for assessing competence. In C. D. Spielberger (Ed.), *Current topics in clinical and community psychology* (Vol. 1, pp. 151–195). New York: Academic Press.

Goldstein, A., & Glick, B. (1987). *Aggression replacement training*. Champaign, IL: Research Press.

Gresham, F. (1986). Conceptual issues in the assessment of social competence in children. In P. Strain, M. Guralnick, & H. Walker (Eds.), *Children's social behavior: Development, assessment, and modification* (pp. 143–179). New York: Academic Press.

Griffiths, R. (1973). A standardized assessment of the work behavior of psychiatric patients. *British Journal of Psychiatry, 123,* 403–408.

Griffiths, R. (1974). Rehabilitation of chronic psychiatric patients. *Psychological Medicine, 4,* 311–325.

Halpern, A. S. (1973). General unemployment and vocational opportunities for EMR individuals. *American Journal of Mental Deficiency, 78,* 123–127.

Halpern, A. S. (1985). Transition: A look at the foundations. *Exceptional Children, 51,* 479–486.

Harris, K. (1982). Cognitive-behavior modification: Application with exceptional students. *Focus on Exceptional Children, 15*(2), 1–16.

Hasazi, S. B., Gordon, L. R., & Roe, C. (1985). Factors associated with the employment status of handicapped youth exiting high school from 1979 to 1983. *Exceptional Children, 51,* 455–469.

Hazel, J. S., Schumaker, J. B., Sherman, J., & Sheldon-Wildgen, J. (1981). The development and evaluation of a group skills training program for court-adjudicated youth. In D. Uppert & S. Ross (Eds.), *Behavioral group therapy,* (pp. 113–152). Champaign, IL: Research Press.

Hazel, J. S., Schumaker, J., Sherman, J., & Sheldon-Wildgen, J. (1982). Group social skills training: A program for court-adjudicated probationary youth. *Criminal Justice and Behavior, 9,* 35–53.

Henggeler, S. (1989). *Delinquency in adolescence*. Beverly Hills, CA: Sage.

Hobbs, N. (1982). *The troubled and troubling child*. San Francisco: Jossey-Bass.

Huesmann, L., Eron, L., Lefkowitz, M., & Walder, L. (1984). Stability of aggression over time and generations. *Developmental Psychology, 20,* 1120–1134.

Hursh, N. (1983). *Diagnostic vocational evaluation with psychiatrically disabled individuals: A national survey.* Boston: Research & Training Center on Mental Health.

Hursh, N., & Kerns, A. (1988). *Vocational evaluation in special education.* Boston: College-Hill.

Ianacone, R., & Leconte, P. (1986). Curriculum-based vocational assessment: A viable response to a school-based service delivery model. *Career Development for Exceptional Individuals, 9,* 113–120.

Janes, C., Hesselbrock, V., Myers, D. G., & Penniman, J. (1979). Problem boys in young adulthood: Teacher's ratings and twelve-year follow-up. *Journal of Youth and Adolescence, 8,* 453–472.

Kavale, K., Forness, S., & Alper, A. (1986). Research in behavioral disorders/emotional disturbance: A survey of subject identification criteria. *Behavioral Disorders, 11,* 159–167.

Kazdin, A. (1979). Situational specificity: The two-edged sword of behavioral assessment. *Behavioral Assessment, 1,* 57–59.

Kazdin, A. (1987a). *Conduct disorders in childhood and adolescence.* Beverly Hills, CA: Sage.

Kazdin, A. (1987b). Treatment of antisocial behavior in children: Current status and future directions. *Psychological Bulletin, 102,* 187–203.

Kelly, J. A., Laughlin, C., Claiborne, M., & Patterson, J. (1979). Group job interview training for unemployed psychiatric patients. *Behavior Therapy, 10,* 299–310.

Kelly, W. J., Salzberg, C. L., Levy, S. M., Warrenfeltz, R. B., Adams, T. W., Crouse, T. R., & Beegle, G. P. (1983). The effects of role-playing and self-monitoring on the generalization of vocational social skills by behaviorally disordered adolescents. *Behavioral Disorders, 9,* 27–35.

Kendall, P., & Braswell, L. (1982). Assessment for cognitive-behavioral interventions in the schools. *School Psychology Review, 11,* 21–31.

Kendall, P., Deardorff, P., & Finch, A. (1977). Empathy and socialization in first and repeat offenders and normals. *Journal of Abnormal Child Psychology, 5,* 93–97.

Kortering, A., & Edgar, E. (1988). Vocational rehabilitation and special education: A need for cooperation. *Rehabilitation Counseling Bulletin, 31,* 178–184.

Kuhlman, H. (1975). The tools of vocational evaluation. *Vocational Evaluation and Work Adjustment Bulletin, 8,* 49–74.

Larson, K. (1984). *The efficacy of social meta-cognitive training for the social adjustment of LD and non-LD delinquents.* Unpublished doctoral dissertation, University of California, Santa Barbara.

Larson, K. A., & Gerber, M. M. (1987). Effects of social metacognitive training for enhancing overt behavior in LD & low achieving delinquents. *Exceptional Children, 54,* 201–211.

Levinson, M., & Neuringer, C. (1971). Problem-solving behavior in suicidal adolescents. *Journal of Consulting and Clinical Psychology, 37,* 433–436.

Loeber, R. (1982). The stability of antisocial and delinquent child behavior: A review. *Child Development, 53,* 1431–1446.

Loeber, R., & Dishion, T. (1983). Early predictors of male delinquency: A review. *Psychological Bulletin, 94,* 68–99.

Loeber, R., & Schmaling, K. (1985a). Empirical evidence for overt and covert patterns of antisocial conduct patterns: A meta-analysis. *Journal of Abnormal Child Psychology, 13,* 337–352.

Loeber, R., & Schmaling, K. (1985b). The utility of differentiating between mixed and pure forms of antisocial child behavior. *Journal of Abnormal Child Psychology, 13,* 315–335.

Lofquist, L., & Dawis, R. (1969). *Adjustment to work: A psychological view of man's problems in a work-oriented society.* New York: Appleton-Century-Crofts.

MacMillan, D., & Kavale, K. (1986). Educational intervention. In H. Quay & J. Werry (Eds.), *Psychopathological disorders of childhood* (3rd ed., pp. 583–621). New York: Wiley.

MacMillan, D., & Morrison, G. (1979). Educational programming. In H. Quay & J. Werry (Eds.), *Psychopathological disorders of childhood* (2nd ed., pp. 411–450). New York: Wiley.

Maddox, M., & Edgar, E. (1988). Maneuvering through the maze: Transition planning for human service agency clients. In P. Dugan & H. Kaney (Eds.), *California transition: Resources and information for transition.* Sacramento: California Department of Education.

Maddox, M., & Webb, S. (1986). Planning for student transitions from juvenile corrections institutions to community schools. *Remedial and Special Education, 7,* 56–61.

Massimo, J., & Shore, M. (1963). The effectiveness of a vocationally oriented psychotherapeutic program for adolescent delinquent boys. *American Journal of Orthopsychiatry, 4,* 634–642.

McCray, P. (1982). *Vocational evaluation and assessment in school settings.* Menomonie, WI: University of Wisconsin-Stout, Stout Vocational Rehabilitation Institute.

McFall, R. (1982). A review and reformulation of the concept of social skills. *Behavioral Assessment, 4*, 1–33.

Meichenbaum, D. (1977). *Cognitive-behavior modification.* New York: Plenum Press.

Mitchell, S., & Rosa, P. (1981). Boyhood behavior problems as precursors of criminality: A fifteen-year follow-up. *Journal of Child Psychology and Psychiatry, 22*, 19–33.

Mithaug, D., Horiuchi, C., & Fanning, P. (1985). A report on the Colorado statewide follow-up survey of special education students. *Exceptional Children, 51*, 397–404.

Neel, R., Meadows, N., Levine, P., & Edgar, E. (1988). What happens after special education: A statewide follow-up study of secondary students who have behavioral disorders. *Behavioral Disorders, 13*, 209–216.

Nelson, C. M., & Kauffman, J. (1977). Educational programming for secondary school age delinquent and maladjusted pupils. *Behavior Disorders, 2*, 102–113.

Niles, W. (1986). Effects of a moral discussion group on delinquent and predelinquent boys. *Journal of Counseling Psychology, 33*, 45–51.

Nishioka-Evans, V. (1987). The Sprague High School project for severely emotionally disturbed youth. *Teaching Research Newsletter, 15*(5).

Ollendick, T., & Hersen, M. (1979). Social skill training for juvenile delinquents. *Behavior Research and Therapy, 17*, 547–554.

Olweus, D. (1977). Aggression and peer acceptance in adolescent boys: Two short-term longitudinal studies of ratings. *Child Development, 48*, 1301–1313.

Olweus, D. (1979). Stability of aggressive reaction patterns in males: A review. *Psychological Bulletin, 86*, 852–875.

Park, H. S., & Gaylord-Ross, R. (1989). Problem solving social skills training in employment settings with mentally retarded youth. (Special issue on supported employment.) *Journal of Applied Behavior Analysis, 22*, 373–380.

Park, H. S., Johnson, B. Tappe, P., Simon, M., Wozniak, T., & Gaylord-Ross, R. (1990). *Relationship and social skill interventions for disabled youth in work settings.* Unpublished manuscript, San Francisco State University, Dept. of Special Education.

Parker, J., & Asher, S. (1987). Peer relations and later personal adjustment: Are low-accepted children at risk? *Psychological Bulletin, 102*, 357–389.

Platt, J., Scura, W., & Hannon, J. (1973). Problem-solving thinking of youthful incarcerated heroin addicts. *Journal of Community Psychology, 43,* 278–281.

Platt, J., Spivack, G., Altman, N., & Altman, D. (1974). Adolescent problem-solving thinking. *Journal of Consulting and Clinical Psychology, 42,* 787–793.

Porter, M., & Stodden, R. (1986). A curriculum-based vocational assessment procedure: Addressing the school-to-work transition needs of secondary schools. *Career Development for Exceptional Individuals, 9,* 121–128.

Porterfield, J., & Gathercole, C. (1985). *The employment of people with mental handicap: Progress towards an ordinary working life.* London: King's Fund Centre.

Pruitt, W. (1976). Vocational evaluation: Yesterday, today, and tomorrow. *Vocational Evaluation and Work Adjustment Bulletin, 9,* 8–16.

Reid, J. (1989). *Prevention, intervention, and understanding of conduct problems of children and adolescents.* Eugene, OR: Oregon Social Learning Center.

Robins, L. N. (1978). Sturdy childhood predictors of adult antisocial behavior: Replications from longitudinal studies. *Psychological Medicine, 8,* 611–622.

Robins, L. N. (1979). Follow-up studies. In H. Quay & J. Werry (Eds.), *Psychopathological disorders of childhood* (2nd ed., pp. 483–514). New York: Wiley.

Roff, J., & Wirt, R. (1984). Childhood aggression and social adjustment as antecedents of delinquency. *Journal of Abnormal Child Psychology, 12,* 111–126.

Romano, J., & Bellack, A. (1980). Social validation of a component model of assertive behavior. *Journal of Consulting and Clinical Psychology, 48,* 478–490.

Salzberg, C., Lignugaris/Kraft, B., & McCuller, G. (1988). Reasons for job loss: A review of employment termination studies of mentally retarded workers. *Research in Developmental Disabilities, 9,* 153–171.

Sarason, I., & Sarason, B. (1981). Teaching cognitive and social skills to high school students. *Journal of Consulting and Clinical Psychology, 49,* 908–918.

Schumaker, J., Hazel, J., Sherman, J., & Sheldon, J. (1982). Social skill performances of learning disabled, non-learning disabled, and delinquent adolescents. *Learning Disabilities Quarterly, 5,* 388–397.

Scruggs, T., & Mastropieri, M. (1985). The first decade of the *Journal of Behavioral Disorders*: A quantitative evaluation. *Behavioral Disorders, 11,* 52–59.

Shore, M., Massimo, J., & Mack, R. (1965). Changes in the perception of interpersonal relationships in successfully treated adolescent delinquent boys. *Journal of Consulting Psychology, 29,* 213–217.

Siegel, S., Gaylord-Ross, R., Greener, K., & Robert, M. (1990). The Career Ladder Program, *Interchange, 10* (3 & 4), 1–3.

Siegel, S., Greener, K., Prieur, J., & Gaylord-Ross, R. (1989). The community vocational training program. *Career Development for Exceptional Individuals, 12,* 48–64.

Sitlington, P., Brolin, D., Clark, G., & Vacanti, J. (1985). Career/vocational ' assessment in the public school setting: The position of the Division on Career Development. *Career Development for Exceptional Individuals, 8,* 3–6.

Slaby, R., & Guerra, N. (1988). Cognitive mediators of aggression in adolescent offenders: Assessment. *Developmental Psychology, 24,* 580–588.

Spence, S. (1981). Validation of social skills of adolescent males in an interview conversation with a previously unknown adult. *Journal of Applied Behavior Analysis, 14,* 159–168.

Spence, S., & Marziller, J. (1979). Social skills training with adolescent male offenders: I. Short-term effects. *Behavior Research and Therapy, 17,* 7–16.

Spence, S., & Marziller, J. (1981). Social skill training with adolescent male offenders: II. Short-term, long-term, and generalized effects. *Behavior Research and Therapy, 19,* 349–368.

Spivack, G., Platt, J., & Shure, M. (1976). *The problem solving approach to adjustment.* San Francisco: Jossey-Bass.

Stodden, R., Ianacone, R., Boone, R., & Bisconer, S. (1987). *Curriculum-based vocational assessment.* Honolulu: Centre Publications.

Strain, P. (1982). Preface. In P. Strain (Ed.), *Social development of exceptional children.* Rockwell, MD: Aspen.

Thornton, H., & Zigmond, N. (1987a). *Post-secondary follow-up of learning disabled and non-handicapped completers of mainstream vocational education programs.* Pittsburgh: University of Pittsburgh.

Thornton, H., & Zigmond, N. (1987b). *Predictors of dropout and unemployment among LD high school youth: The holding power of secondary vocational education for LD students.* Pittsburgh: University of Pittsburgh.

Thornton, H., & Zigmond, N. (1988). Secondary vocational training for LD students and its relationship to school completion status and post school outcomes. *Illinois Schools Journal, 67*(2), 37–54.

Trower, P. (1984). A radical critique and reformulation: From organism to agent. In P. Trower (Ed.), *Radical approaches to social skills training* (pp. 47–88). New York: Croom Helm.

Vocational Evaluation and Work Adjustment Association. (1975). *VEWAA-CARF vocational evaluation and work adjustment standards.* Menomonie, WI: University of Wisconsin-Stout, Stout Vocational Rehabilitation Institute.

Wagner, M., & Shaver, D. (1989). *Educational programs and achievements of secondary special education students: Findings from the National Longitudinal Transition Study.* Menlo Park, CA: SRI International.

Warrenfeltz, R., Kelly, W., Salzberg, C., Beegle, C., Levy, S., Adams, T., & Crouse, T. (1981). Social skills training of behavior disordered adolescents with self-monitoring to promote generalization to a vocational setting. *Behavioral Disorders, 7,* 18–27.

Watts, F. (1978). A study of work behavior in a psychiatric unit. *British Journal of Clinical Psychology, 17,* 85–92.

Will, M. (1984). *OSERS program for the transition of youth with handicaps from school to working life.* Washington, DC: Office of Special Education and Rehabilitation Services.

CEC Mini-Library
Working with Behavioral Disorders

Edited by Lyndal M. Bullock and Robert B. Rutherford, Jr.

A set of nine books developed with the practitioner in mind.

Use this Mini-Library as a reference to help staff understand the problems of specific groups of youngsters with behavioral problems.

- *Teaching Students with Behavioral Disorders: Basic Questions and Answers.* Timothy J. Lewis, Juane Heflin, & Samuel A. DiGangi. No. P337. 1991. 37 pages.

- *Conduct Disorders and Social Maladjustments: Policies, Politics, and Programming.* Frank H. Wood, Christine O. Cheney, Daniel H. Cline, Kristina Sampson, Carl R. Smith, & Eleanor C. Guetzloe. No. P338. 1991. 27 pages.

- *Behaviorally Disordered? Assessment for Identification and Instruction.* Bob Algozzine, Kathy Ruhl, & Roberta Ramsey, No. P339. 1991. 37 pages.

- *Preparing to Integrate Students with Behavioral Disorders.* Robert A. Gable, Virginia K. Laycock, Sharon A. Maroney, & Carl R. Smith. No. P340. 1991. 35 pages

- *Teaching Young Children with Behavioral Disorders.* Mary Kay Zabel. No. P341. 1991. 25 pages.

- *Reducing Undesirable Behaviors.* Edited by Lewis Polsgrove. No. P342. 1991. 33 pages.

- *Social Skills for Students with Autism.* Richard L. Simpson, Brenda Smith Myles, Gary M. Sasso, & Debra M. Kamps. No. P343. 1991. 23 pages.

- *Special Education in Juvenile Corrections.* Peter E. Leone, Robert B. Rutherford, Jr., & C. Michael Nelson. No. P344. 1991. 26 pages.

- *Moving On: Transitions for Youth with Behavioral Disorders.* Michael Bullis & Robert Gaylord-Ross. No. P345. 1991. 52 pages.

Save 10% by ordering the entire library, No. P346, 1991. Call for the most current price information, 703/264-9467.

Send orders to:
The Council for Exceptional Children, Dept. K10350
1920 Association Drive, Reston VA 22091-1589